Collins
easy learning

Thai
phrasebook

Consultant
Tasneeya Sae-Mak

First published 2007
This edition published 2010
Copyright © HarperCollins Publishers
Reprint 10 9 8 7 6 5 4 3 2 1 0
Typeset by Davidson Pre-Press, Glasgow
Printed in Malaysia for Imago

www.collinslanguage.com

ISBN 978-0-00-736450-3

Using your phrasebook

Your *Collins Gem Phrasebook* is designed to help you locate the exact phrase you need, when you need it, whether on holiday or for business. If you want to adapt the phrases, you can easily see where to substitute your own words using the dictionary section, and the clear, full-colour layout gives you direct access to the different topics.

The Gem Phrasebook includes:
• Over 70 topics arranged thematically. Each phrase is accompanied by a simple pronunciation guide which eliminates any problems pronouncing foreign words.

• A top ten tips section to safeguard against any cultural faux pas, giving essential dos and don'ts for situations involving local customs or etiquette.

• Practical hints to make your stay trouble free, showing you where to go and what to do when dealing with everyday matters such as travel or hotels and offering valuable tourist information.

- Face to face sections so that you understand what is being said to you. These example mini-dialogues give you a good idea of what to expect from a real conversation.

- Common announcements and messages you may hear, ensuring that you never miss the important information you need to know when out and about.

- A clearly laid-out dictionary means you will never be stuck for words.

- A basic grammar section which will enable you to build on your phrases.

- A list of public holidays to avoid being caught out by unexpected opening and closing hours, and to make sure you don't miss the celebrations!

It's worth spending time before you embark on your travels just looking through the topics to see what is covered and becoming familiar with what might be said to you.

Whatever the situation, your *Gem Phrasebook* is sure to help!

Contents

Pronouncing Thai

Thai is a tonal language, which means that it needs to be pronounced in the correct tone. Otherwise miscommunication may occur. There are five tones in the Thai language:

Mid Tone

This is spoken in an ordinary tone of voice without any inflection. It sounds like the tone used in ordinary English conversation. There is no symbol to represent this tone.

มา	maa	to come
ดี	dii	good
ใจ	jai	heart
ไกล	glai	far

Low Tone

This is a level of tone with no inflection. However, it sounds lower in pitch than the mid tone. The symbol used in this phrasebook is ` .

หนึ่ง	nùng	one
จะ	jà	will
ใส่	sài	to wear
ข่าว	kàao	news

The Falling Tone

A pronounced, emphasized tone with a falling inflection. It is similar to the tone used in English to denote emphasis. The symbol used in this phrasebook is ^.

ไม่	mâi	no, not
ข้าว	kâao	rice
ใช่	châi	correct
นี่	nîi	this

High Tone

This level of tone is above the level of normal tone. It is pronounced in the same way as asking a question in the English language. The symbol used in this phrasebook is ´.

ม้า	máa	horse
วัด	wát	temple
รัก	rák	to love
รู้	rúu	to know

Rising Tone

This level of tone is similar to the tone used in English to denote surprise. The symbol used in this phrasebook is ˇ.

หมา	mǎa	dog
ไหม	mǎi	silk
ขาว	kǎao	white
หนังสือ	nǎngsǔu	book

Vowels

• •

There are two types of vowel: short and long. Short vowels are cut off at the end. Long vowels are drawn out. A long vowel sound is represented by a double letter or a combination of two letters. A short vowel sound is represented by a single letter or a single letter followed by a colon.

Short and Long vowels

• •

a	as in	**a**way
aa	as in	f**a**ther
i	as in	t**i**p
ii	as in	b**ee**
u	as in	g**oo**d
uu	as in	r**u**le
e	as in	g**e**t
ee	as in	p**a**le
o	as in	b**oa**t
oo	as in	g**o**
o	as in	**aw**kward
o	as in	f**or**
a:	as in	h**a**zard
ae	as **a** in	h**a**ng
u:	as **e** in	th**e**
ur	as **u** in	b**ur**n

Consonants

• •

The Thai language has 44 consonants and 32 vowel characters. However, there are actually only 20 consonant sounds. In the following list are the consonants that are pronounced in the same way as in English.

ก	= **g** as in **g**ood
ข ค ฆ	= **k** as in **k**ing
จ	= **j** as in **J**anuary
ช ส, ษ, ศ	= **s** as in **s**eek
ด, ฎ	= **d** as in **d**oor
บ	= **b** as in **b**aby
ม	= **m** as in **m**other
น ณ	= **n** as in **n**oun
ล ฬ	= **l** as in **l**ove
ร	= **r** as in **r**oll
ว	= **w** as in **w**oman
ท ธ	= **t** as in **t**ime
ย, ญ	= **y** as in **y**ou
ฟ	= **f** as in **f**un
ห ฮ	= **h** as in **h**oney

11

The following are a few sounds that are difficult to pronounce.

ฎ �	= **dt** as in s**t**op
ป	= **bp** as in s**p**ain
ช ฌ ฌ	= **ch** as in **ch**ange
ง	= **ng** as in ri**ng**ing

The '**dt**' tone is the sound between '**d**' and '**t**'. Similarly, the '**bp**' tone is the sound between '**b**' and '**p**'. Thai people often do not differentiate between the sounds '**r**' and '**l**': these two sounds are usually pronouced in the same tone. The '**ng**' sound in English normally occurs at the end of words. Unlike in English, '**ng**' is often used at the beginning of Thai words.

Top ten tips

1 Thailand is a Buddhist country. You should dress appropriately when visiting a Buddhist temple. Slippers, shorts, miniskirts and tank tops are not permitted, and shoes should be removed before entering.

2 Thai people hold their King and Queen in great reverence. The national anthem is played twice a day (at 8.00 am and again at 6.00 pm), and also before a film at the cinema. Everyone shows their respect by standing while the anthem is playing, and you will be expected to do the same.

3 It is polite to call Thai people by their first name and add the word **Khun** before it. The word **Khun** can be used for both men and women. It is not used for children.

4 It is normal for people to stand or sit very close to each other when talking, which may be closer than you're used to. Pulling away from your counterpart may be regarded as unfriendly.

5   Public shows of intimacy between men and women are not approved of.

6   Never touch a person's head. Thai people believe that the head is the noblest part of the body.

7   Never use your feet to point things out or to touch any part of another person's body. That is considered very rude.

8   You will be expected to take your shoes off when you enter a Thai house.

9   If you are picking up food with your hands, use your right hand.

10 Women are not allowed to touch a Buddhist monk.

Talking to people

Hello/goodbye, yes/no

It is easy to remember how to say hello, good morning, good afternoon and good evening in Thai as the language uses the words สวัสดีครับ/ค่ะ sà-wad-dii krab/ka for any occasion except goodnight.

Goodbye	ลานะครับ/ค่ะ laa na krab/ká
Farewell	ลาก่อนครับ/ค่ะ la kòrn krab/ká
See you again	พบกันใหม่ครับ/ค่ะ pob kan mài krab/ká
See you tomorrow	พบกันพรุ่งนี้ pob-kan-prûng níi
Yes	ใช่ครับ/ค่ะ châi krab/ká
No	ไม่ใช่ครับ/ค่ะ mâi châi krab/ká

Please	กรุณา, โปรด
	ga-ru-naa, pròot
Thank you	ขอบคุณครับ/ค่ะ
	kòrb kun-krab/ká
Thanks	ขอบใจ
	korb-jai
Sorry!	ขอโทษครับ/ค่ะ
	kör tôot krab/ká!
Excuse me!	ประทานโทษครับ/ค่ะ
	bpra-taan- tôot krab/ká!
I don't understand	ผม/ดิฉันไม่เข้าใจ
	pöm/di-chan mâi kâo-jai
I cannot speak Thai	ผม / ดิฉัน พูดภาษาไทยไม่ได้
	pöm/di-chanpûud paa-säa thai mâi dâi

Key phrases

• •

| Where is...? | ที่ไหน |
| | tîi näi...? |

Where is the nearest bank?	ธนาคารที่ใกล้ที่สุดอยู่ที่ไหน
	ta-naa-kaan tîi glâi tîi sut yùu tîi näi?
Where is the toilet?	ห้องสุขาอยู่ที่ไหน
	hô:ng su-käa yùu tîi näi?
How...?	เท่าไหร่
	tâo-rài?
How much does it cost?	อันนี้เท่าไหร่ครับ/คะ
	an níi tâo-rài krab/ká?
Is it included...?	มันรวมกับ...
	man ruam kàb...?
When is/are...?	เมื่อไหร่
	mûa-rài...?
When is breakfast?	อาหารเช้าเสริฟตอนกี่โมง
	aa-häan cháao surp dtorn gìi moong?
When are we going?	เราจะไปเมื่อไหร่
	rao ja bpai mûa-rài?
What time is it?	กี่โมงแล้ว
	gìi moong láew?
At what time...?	ตอนกี่โมง
	dtorn gìi moong?

What is it?	นี่คืออะไร
	nîi kuu a-rai?
Which one?	อันไหน
	an-nǎi?
Why?	ทำไม
	tam mai?
Please leave!	กรุณาออกไป
	ga-ru-naa òrk bpai!
Do you have...?	คุณมี
	khun mii ... mái?
I would like...	ผม/ดิฉัน ต้องการ...
	pöm dtô:ng gaan...
I would like a bottle of beer	ผมต้องการเบียร์หนึ่งขวด
	pöm dtô:ng gaan beer nùng kùat
Can I...?	ขอผม/ดิฉัน ... ได้ไหม
	kör pöm/di-chan ... dâai mái?
Can I use your phone?	ขอผมใช้โทรศัพท์ได้ไหม
	kör pöm chái too-rá-sàp dâai mái?
Can I smoke?	ขอผมสูบบุหรี่ได้ไหม
	kör pöm sùub burìi dâai mái?
There is/are...	ที่นี่มี...
	tîi nîi mii...
There isn't...	ที่นี่ไม่มี...
	tîi nîi mâi mii...

Signs and notices

เปิด	bpùrt	open
ปิด	bpìd	closed
สุภาพสตรี	sù-pâap-sà-dtrii	Ladies
สุภาพบุรุษ	sù-pâap-bu-rut	Gentlemen
บริการตนเอง	bo:-ri-gaan-dtua-eeng	self-service
ผลัก	plàk	push
ดึง	dung	pull
ที่จ่ายเงิน	tîi jàai ngurn	cash desk
น้ำดื่ม	náam dùum	drinking water
ห้องน้ำ/สุขา	hô:ng-náam/su-käa	toilets
ว่าง	wâang	vacant
ไม่ว่าง	mâi wâang	engaged
ห้องฉุกเฉิน	hô:ng chùk chürn	emergency room

ปฐมพยาบาล	bpà-töm pa-yaa-baan	first aid
เต็ม	dtem	full
หยุด	yùt	stop
ปิดซ่อม	bpìd sô:m	out of order
ให้เช่า	hâi châo	for rent
ขาย	käai	for sale
ลดราคา	lót raa-kaa	sales
ใต้ถุน	dtâai tün	basement
ชั้นล่าง	chán lâang	ground floor
ทางเข้า	taang kâo	entrance
ที่ขายตั๋ว	tïi käai dtüa	ticket office
สถานีตำรวจ	sa-täa-nii dtam-rùat	police station
ของหาย	kö:ng häai	lost property
ขาออก	käa-òrk	departures
ขาเข้า	käa-kâo	arrivals
ห้าม	hâam	prohibited

กระเป๋าเดินทางที่ถูกลืม	grà-bpǎo-durn-taang tîi tùuk luum	left luggage
ส่วนบุคคล	sùan buk-kol	private
ร้อน	rórn	hot
หนาว/เย็น	nǎao/yen	cold
อันตราย	an-dta-raai	danger
ห้ามสูบบุหรี่	hâam sùub-bu-rìi	no smoking
กรุณาอย่าจับ	ka-ru-naa yàa jàb	do not touch
ทางออก	taang-òrk	exit
ห้องเปลี่ยนเสื้อผ้า	hô:ng bplìan sûa-pâa	changing room
ห้องน้ำ	hô:ng náam	bathroom
ระวัง	ra-wang	caution
ข้อมูล	kôr-moon	information
สอบถาม	sòrb-thǎam	enquiries

Polite expressions

Thailand is a land of smiles and Thai people are kind and friendly. One easy way to add politeness to a sentence is to add the word ครับ krab (for men/boys) or คะ ká (for women/girls) at the end of the sentence. For example:

How are you?	สบายดีไหมครับ
(to be said by a man/boy)	sà baai dii mái krab?
(to be said by a woman/girl)	สบายดีไหมคะ
	sà baai dii mái ká?

Traditionally, Thai people greet each other with the ไหว้ wai **action**, which involves pressing the palms together in front of the chest and bowing the head a little, and saying 'sà-wàd-dii krab/ká.'

How do you do?	สบายดีไหมครับ/คะ
	sà baai dii mái krab/ká?
I am fine	ผม/ดิฉัน สบายดี
	pöm/di-chan sà baai dii
Thank you	ขอบคุณ
	kòrb kun

My name is...	ผม/ดิฉัน ชื่อ...
	pöm/di-chan chûu...
Welcome!	ยินดีต้อนรับ
	yindii dtôrn rab
Yes, Sir	ครับ/ค่ะ
	krab/ká
Pardon me/	ขอโทษครับ/คะ
Excuse me	kör toot krab/ká
This is...	นี่คือ...
	nîi kuu...
This is my	นี่คือภรรยา (สามี)
husband (wife)	ของผม/ดิฉัน
	nîi kuu panrayaa (säamii) kö:ng
	pöm/dichan
Enjoy your meal!	ทานอาหารให้อร่อย
	นะครับ/คะ
	taan aa-häan hâi aròy na krab/ká!
Pleased to meet	ยินดีที่ได้รู้จักครับ/ค่ะ
you	yin dii tîi dâai rú:u-jàk krab/ká
The meal was	อาหารอร่อยมากครับ/ค่ะ
delicious	aa-häan aròy mâak krab/ká
Thank you very	ขอบคุณมากครับ/ค่ะ
much	kòrb kun mâak krab/ká

Have a good trip!	เดินทางให้สนุกครับ/ค่ะ
	durn taang hâi sa-nuk krab/ká!
Enjoy your holiday!	เที่ยวให้สนุกนะครับ/ค่ะ
	tieew hâi sanuk na krab/ká!

Celebrations

Happy birthday!	สุขสันต์วันเกิด
	sùk-sän wan gùrt!
Congratulations!	ยินดีด้วยครับ/ค่ะ
	yin dii dôay krab/ká!
Cheers! (when you raise your glass)	ไชโย
	chai-yo!
Happy New Year!	สวัสดีปีใหม่
	sa-wad-dii bpii mài!

Making friends

| Hello my name is... | สวัสดีครับ/ค่ะ ผม/ดิฉัน ชื่อ... |
| | sa-wad-dii krab/ká pöm/di-chan chûu... |

> **Public holidays** (p 163)

What is your name?	คุณชื่ออะไรครับ/คะ khun chûu a-rai krab/ka?
Where are you from?	คุณมาจากประเทศอะไร khun maa jàak bpra têet a-rai?
I am from England	ผม/ดิฉัน มาจากประเทศ อังกฤษ pöm/di-chan maa jàak bpra têet ang-grìt
Nice to meet you	ยินดีที่ได้รู้จักคุณ yindii tîi dâai rúu jàk
How old are you?	คุณอายุเท่าไหร่ khun aa-yú tâo-rài?
I'm ... years old	ผม/ดิฉัน อายุ ... ปี pöm/di-chan aa-yú ... bpii
Where do you live?	คุณอยู่ที่ไหน khun yùu tîi näi?
I live in London	ผม/ดิฉัน อยู่ในลอนดอน pöm/di-chan yùu tîi london
Are you married?	คุณแต่งงานแล้วหรือยัง khun dtàeng-ngaan láew rüu yang?
Do you have any children?	คุณมีลูกหรือยัง khun mii lûuk rüu yang?
I have children	ผม/ดิฉัน มีลูกแล้ว pöm/di-chan mii lûuk láew

I don't have children	ผม/ดิฉัน ไม่มีลูก
	pöm/di-chan mâi mii lûuk
I have a boyfriend/ girlfriend	ผม/ดิฉัน มีแฟนแล้ว
	pöm/di-chan mii faen láew
I'm single	ผม/ดิฉัน เป็นโสด
	pöm/di-chan bpen sòot
I'm married	ผม/ดิฉัน แต่งงานแล้ว
	pöm/di-chan dtàeng-ngaan láew
I'm divorced	ผม/ดิฉัน เป็นหม้าย
	pöm/di-chan bpen mâai

Work

. . . .

What is your job?	คุณทำงานอะไร
	khun tam-ngaan a-rai?
Do you enjoy it?	คุณชอบงานของคุณไหม
	khun chôrb ngaan kö:ng khun mái?
I'm a doctor	ผม/ดิฉัน เป็นหมอ
	pöm/di-chan bpen mör
I'm a teacher	ผม/ดิฉัน เป็นครู
	pöm/di-chan bpen kruu

 > **Leisure/beach** (p 79) > **Sport** (p 85)

I'm a nurse	ผม/ดิฉัน เป็น บุรุษพยาบาล/พยาบาล
	pöm/di-chan bpen bu-rut pa-yaa-baan/pa-yaa-baan
I work in a shop	ผม/ดิฉัน ทำงานในร้านค้า
	pöm/di-chan tam-ngaan nai ráan káa
I work in a factory	ผม/ดิฉัน ทำงานในโรงงาน
	pöm/di-chan tam-ngaan nai roong-ngaan
I work in a bank	ผม/ดิฉัน ทำงานในธนาคาร
	pöm/di-chan tam-ngaan nai ta-naa-kaan
I work from home	ผม/ดิฉัน ทำงานที่บ้าน
	pöm/di-chan tam-ngaan tîi bâan

Work

> **Making friends** (p 24)

Weather

สดใส sòd-säi	clear
ฝนตก fön-dtòk	rainy
หนาว näao	cold
ร้อน rórn	hot
ฟ้าใส fáa säi	sunny
ลมแรง lom-raeng	windy
พยากรณ์อากาศ pa-yaa-korn aa-gàat	weather forecast

It's sunny   แดดออก
                 dàed òrk

It's raining   ฝนกำลังตก
                 fön gamlang dtòk

It's windy   ลมแรงทีเดียว
                 lom-raeng tii-diao

It's very hot   ร้อนมากมาก
                 rórn mâak mâak

What is the temperature?	อุณหภูมิเท่าไหร่ un-hà-puum tâo rài?
What is the weather forecast for tomorrow?	พรุ่งนี้อากาศจะเป็นอย่างไร prûng níi aa-gàat ja bpen yaang-rài?
Does it get cool at night?	ตอนกลางคืนอากาศหนาวไหม dtorn glaang-kuun aa-gàat näao mái?
Will there be a storm?	จะมีพายุไหม ja mii paa-yu mái?
What beautiful weather!	อากาศดีจริงจริง aa-gàat dii jing jing!
What awful weather!	อากาศไม่ดี aa-gàat mâi dii!

Getting around

Asking the way

ซ้าย sáai	left
ขวา kwäa	right
ตรงไป dtrong bpai	straight on
ตรงข้ามกับ dtrong kâam kàp	opposite
ติดกับ dtìd kàp	next to
ไฟจราจร fai ja-raa-jorn	traffic lights
ตรงหัวมุม dtrong hüa mum	at the corner

A ขอโทษครับ/ค่ะ
   ที่ทำการไปรษณีย์อยู่ที่ไหนครับ/คะ
kör-tôot krab/ka tîi tam-gaanbprai-sa-nii yùu tîi näi
   krab/ka?
Excuse me. Where is the post office?

B เดินตรงไป แล้วเลี้ยวขวา/ซ้าย ตรงหัวมุม
durn dtrong bpai láew líao kwäa/sáai dtrong hüa-mum
Keep straight on and turn right/left at the corner

A ไกลไหมครับ/คะ
glai mái krab/ká?
Is it far?

B ไม่ไกลครับ/ค่ะ ห่างแค่ 200 เมตร/
   2 นาที
mâi glai krab/ka hàang kâe so:ng-ro:y met/
   so:ng naa-tii
No. Only 200 metres/2 minutes away

A ขอบคุณครับ/ค่ะ
kòrb kun - krab/ká
Thank you

B ไม่เป็นไรครับ/ค่ะ
mâi bpen rai krab/ka
You are welcome

Where is...?	…อยู่ไหน
	…yùu näi?
Where is the museum?	พิพิธภัณฑ์อยู่ไหน
	pi-pit-ta-pan yùu näi?
How do I get...?	ผม/ดิฉัน จะไป … ได้อย่างไร
	pöm/di-chan ja bpai … dâai yàang rai?
How do I get to the museum?	ผม/ดิฉัน จะไปพิพิธภัณฑ์ ได้อย่างไร
	pöm/di-chan ja bpai pi-pit-ta-pan dâi yàang rai?
to the coach station	ไปท่ารถขนส่ง
	bpai tâa rót kön sòng
to the beach	ไปที่ชายหาด
	bpai tîi chaai-hàat
to my hotel	ไปที่โรงแรมของฉัน
	bpai tîi roong-raem kö:ng chan

เลี้ยวซ้าย líao sáai	Turn left
เลี้ยวขวา líao kwäa	Turn right
เดินตรงไป durn dtrong bpai	Keep straight on
ใกล้ใกล้ glâi glâi	Closer to

Bus and coach

Buses and coaches are the cheapest way to travel in Thailand. Bus services are provided by the government. If you plan to travel around Bangkok by bus, you can get a free copy of the city's maps from the TAT (Tourism Authority of Thailand) counter at the airport. Coach services are operated by both the government and private companies. The private companies charge a little more than the government-run coach service does, but they are faster and more comfortable.

> **Maps and guides** (p 71)

ท่ารถเมล์ tâa rót meey	bus stop
ท่ารถขนส่ง tâa rót kön sòng	coach station
ตั๋ว dtüa	ticket

FACE TO FACE

A ขอโทษครับ/ค่ะ รถไปเชียงใหม่ออกเวลา 10 โมงคันไหนครับ/คะ

kör-tôot krab/ka rót bpai chiang mai ork wei-laa sìp moong kan näi krab/ka?

Excuse me. Which one is the 10 o'clock Chiang Mai bus?

B คันทางซ้าย/ขวา สีน้ำเงินครับ/ค่ะ

kan taang sáai/kwäa sïi náam-ngurn krab/ká

The one on the right/left. The blue bus.

| Where is the coach station? | ท่ารถขนส่งอยู่ที่ไหนครับ/คะ
tâa rót kön sòng yùu näi krab/ká? |
| I am going to... | ผม/ดิฉัน กำลังจะไป...
pöm/dichan kamlang ja bpai... |

34

Is there a bus to...?	**มีรถไป … ไหมครับ/คะ**
	mii rót bpai … mái krab/ká?
Does it go to...?	**มันไปถึง … ไหมครับ/ค่ะ**
	man bpai tüng … mái krab/ká?
It goes to...	**มันไปถึง…**
	man bpai tüng…
the airport	**ท่าอากาศยาน**
	bpai tâa aa-gàat-sa-yaan
the beach	**ชายหาด**
	bpai chaai-hàat
the shopping centre	**ศูนย์การค้า**
	bpai süun gaan káa
1 ticket	**ตั๋วหนึ่งใบ**
	dtüa nùng bai
2 tickets	**ตั๋วสองใบ**
	dtüa sö:ng bai
3 tickets	**ตั๋วสามใบ**
	dtüa säam bai
When is the next bus?	**รถเที่ยวหน้ากี่โมงครับ/ คะ**
	rót tîew nâa kìi moong krab/ká?

Bus and coach

ไม่มีรถบริการเหลือ แล้วครับ/ค่ะ mâi mii rót bo:-ri- gaan láew krab/ká	There is no bus
คุณต้องไปรถแท็กซี่ khun tô:ng bpai rót tá:k-sîi	You must take a taxi
ตั๋วขายหมดแล้วครับ/ค่ะ dtüa käai mòt láew krab/ká	The tickets are sold out

Metro/Sky train

Bangkok is the only city that has metro and sky train services which run from 6 am to 12 pm. Fares range from 14 – 36 baht. Monthly tickets are also available.

ทางเข้า	taang kâo	entrance
ทางออก	taang-òrk	way out

Where is the nearest metro station?	สถานีรถไฟใต้ดินที่ใกล้ที่ สุดอยู่ที่ไหนครับ/ค่ะ sa-täa-nii rót fai dtâi din tîi glâi tîi sut yùu tîi näi krab/ká?

36

How does the ticket machine work?	เครื่องขายตั๋วอัตโนมัติใช้ยังไงครับ/คะ
	krûang käai dtüa àt-tà-noo-mát chái yang ngai krab/ká?
Do you have a map of the metro?	คุณมีแผนที่ของรถไฟใต้ดินไหมครับ/คะ
	khun mii päen-tîi rót fai dtâi din mái krab/ká?
I'm going to...	ผมจะไป...
	pöm ja bpai...
How do I/we get to...?	ผม/พวกเรา จะไป ... ไดอย่างไร
	pöm/puag-rao ja bpai ... dâai yang rai?
Do I have to change?	ผมต้องเปลี่ยนรถไหม
	pöm dtô:ng bplian rót mái?
What is the next stop?	ป้ายหน้าอะไรครับ/คะ
	bpâi nâa a-rai krab/ká?
Excuse me. I'm getting off here	ขอโทษครับ/ค่ะ ผม/ดิฉัน จะลงป้ายนี้
	kör-tôot krab/ká pöm/di-chan ja long bpâi níi
Please let me through	ขอทางด้วยครับ/ค่ะ
	kör taang dûai krab/ká

Metro/Sky train

> **Luggage** (p 99)

Train

Train services are offered throughout the country and the fares are very reasonable. The train centre in Bangkok is Hualamphong Station หัวลำโพง hua-lam-phong.

Thai	English
สถานี sa-täa-nii	station
รถไฟ rót fai	train
ชานชาลา chaan-chaa-laa	platform
ที่นั่ง tîi nâng	seat
ตั๋ว dtüa	ticket
ที่ขายตั๋ว tîi käai dtüa	booking office
ตารางเวลา dtaa-raang wee-laa	timetable
เปลี่ยนเส้นทาง bplian sên taang	connection

> **Luggage** (p 99)

A รถไฟไปสงขลาเที่ยวหน้ากี่โมงครับ/คะ
rót fai bpai söng-kläa tîao nâa gìi moong krab/ka?
When is the next train to Song Khla?

B สิบโมง
sìp moong
At 10 o'clock

A ซื้อตั๋วสามใบ
súu dtüa säam bai
3 tickets please

B ตั๋วเที่ยวเดียวหรือไปกลับ
dtüa tîao diao rüu bpai glàb?
Single or return?

A ไปกลับ
bpai glàb
Return, please

Where is the station?	สถานีรถไฟอยู่ไหน sa-täa-nii rót fai yùu näi?
a single	เที่ยวเดียว tîao diao

2 singles	เที่ยวเดียวสองใบ
	tîao diao sö:ng bai
a single to Lum Pang	ตั๋วเที่ยวเดียวหนึ่งใบไปลำปาง
	dtüa tîao diao nùng bai bpai lum-pang
2 singles to Sukothai	ตั๋วเที่ยวเดียวสองใบไปสุโขทัย
	dtüa tîao diao sö:ng bai bpai su-köo-tai
a return	ตั๋วไปกลับ
	dtüa bpai glàb
2 returns	ตั๋วไปกลับสองใบ
	dtüa bpai glàb sö:ng bai
1 adult	ผู้ใหญ่หนึ่งคน
	pûu yài nùng kon
2 children	เด็กสองคน
	dèk sö:ng kon
2 adults	ผู้ใหญ่สองคน
	pûu yài sö:ng kon
first class	ชั้นหนึ่ง
	chán nùng

second class	ชั้นสอง
	chán sö:ng
smoking	สูบบุหรี่ได้
	sùub burii dâai
non-smoking	ห้ามสูบบุหรี่
	hâam sùub burii
I want to book a seat	ฉันต้องการจองตั๋วหนึ่งใบ
	chan tô:ng gaan jorng dtüa nùng bai
Which platform?	ชานชาลาไหน
	chaan-chaa-laa näi?
When does it get to Nakhon Pathom?	จะไปถึงนครปฐมกี่โมง
	. bpai tüng na-korn-bpa-töm gìi moong?
When does it leave?	มันจะออกตอนกี่โมง
	man ja òrk dtorn gìi moong?
When does it arrive?	มันไปถึงตอนกี่โมง
	man bpai tüng dtorn gìi moong?
Is this seat free?	ที่นั่งนี้ว่างไหม
	tîi nâng níi wâang mái?
Excuse me!	ขอโทษ
	kör-tôot!

Taxi

.

Taxi services in Bangkok are very convenient, and you can hire one by either hailing it from the street or telephoning the service provider. The telephones used to call taxi services are installed at most of the bus stops in Bangkok.

Where can I get a taxi?	ฉันจะเรียกแท็กซี่ได้ที่ไหน
	chan ja rîak tá:k-sîi dâai tîi näi?
I want to go to...	ผม/ดิฉัน ต้องการไปที่...
	pöm/di-chan tô:ng gaan bpai tîi...
How much is it?	เท่าใหร่
	tâo rài?
To the airport, please	ไปสนามบิน
	bpai sà-näam-bin
To the beach, please	ไปชายหาด
	bpai chaai-hàat
Please stop here	จอดตรงนี้
	jòrt dtrong níi
Please wait	ช่วยรอตรงนี้
	chûai ror dtrong níi

> **Luggage** (p 99)

It's too expensive	มันแพงมาก
	man paeng mâak
I haven't got any change	ฉันไม่มีเศษสตางค์
	chan mâi mii sèet-sa-taang
Keep the change	ไม่ต้องคืนตังทอน
	mâi dtô:ng kuun dtang torn

Boat

In Bangkok there are several types of boat services on the Chao Phraya River. The motorboat service runs between Wat Ratchasingkhon and Nonthaburi province. The Chao Phraya Tourist boat stops at major places in Bangkok, such as the Grand Palace, Wat Pho and Chinatown. The Long-tail Boat offers a Chao Phraya River tour for small private groups.

Thai		English
ที่ขายตั๋ว	tîi käai dtüa	ticket office
ตารางเวลา dtaa-raang wee-laa		timetable
ขาเข้า	käa-kâo	arrival
ขาออก	käa-òrk	departure

When is the next boat?	เรือเที่ยวหน้ามาเมื่อใหร่
	rua tîao nâa maa mûa rai?
When is the last boat?	เรือเที่ยวสุดท้ายตอนกี่โมง
	rua tîao sut táai dtorn gìi moong?
We want to go to...	เราต้องการจะไป...
	rao dtô:ng gaan ja bpai...
Is there a timetable?	ตารางเวลาเรืออยู่ที่ไหน
	dtaa-raang wee-laa rua yùu tîi näi?
When does the boat leave?	เรือจะออกตอนกี่โมง
	rua ja òrk dtorn gìi moong?
How long does it take?	ใช้เวลานานเท่าไหร่
	chái wee-laa naan tâo rài?

Air travel

สนามบิน sà-näam-bin	airport
ประตู bpra-dtuu	gate
ขาเข้า käa-kâo	arrivals
ขาออก käa-òrk	departures
เที่ยวบิน tîao bin	flight

ภายในประเทศ paai-nai bpra-têet	domestic
นานาชาติ naa-naa- châat	international
ข้อมูล kôr-muun	information

To the airport, please	ไปสนามบิน bpai sà-näam-bin

My flight is at ... o'clock	เครื่องผม/
	   ดิฉัน ออกตอน ...โมง
	krûang pöm/di-chan òrk
	   dtorn ... moong

How much is it to the airport?	ไปสนามบินเท่าไหร่ bpai sà-näam-bin tâo rài?
How much is it to the town centre?	ไปใจกลางเมืองเท่าไหร่ bpai jai glaang muang tâo rài?
When will the flight leave?	เครื่องจะออกเมื่อไหร่ krûang ja òrk mûa rai?

YOU MAY HEAR...

ไปที่ประตูเบอร์... bpai tîi bpra dtuu bur...	Go to gate number...

Air travel

Customs control

The import, export, possession or use of drugs is forbidden and penalties for offenders are severe.

Getting around

หนังสือเดินทาง năng-sŭu-durn-taang	passport
ศุลกากร sŭn-la-gaa-gorn	customs
ของมึนเมา/ ยาสูบ kŏ:ng mun mao/yaa-sùub	alcohol/ tobacco

Do I have to pay duty on this?	อันนี้ฉันต้องเสียภาษีไหม an níi chan dtô:ng sĭa paa-sĭi mài?
It is my medicine	มันเป็นยาของฉัน man bpen yaa kŏ:ng chan
The children are on this passport	เด็ก ๆ รวมอยู่ในหนังสือ เดินทางเล่มนี้ dèk dèk ruam yùu nai năng-sŭu-durn-taang lêm níi
I bought this duty-free	ฉันซื้ออันนี้จากร้านสินค้า ปลอดภาษี chan súu an níi jàak ráan sĭn-káa bplòrt paa-sĭi

Driving

Car hire

Big cities such as Bangkok, Chiang Mai, Pattaya and Phuket have cars and motorcycles for rent. Most of the car rental companies have their offices in medium to large hotels.

หนังสือประกันภัย	insurance documents
näng-süu bpra-gan pai	
ใบขับขี่ bai-kàp-kìi	driving licence

I want to hire a car	ฉันต้องการเช่ารถ
	chan dtô:ng gaan châo rót
with automatic gears	ขอเกียร์ออโตเมติก
	kör gia or-dtoo-mee-dtik
for 1 day	หนึ่งวัน
	nùng wan
for 2 days	สองวัน
	sö:ng wan

How much is it?	**เท่าไหร่**
	tâo rài?
Is insurance included?	**รวมค่าประกันไหม**
	ruam kâa bpra-gan mái?
Is there a deposit to pay?	**ต้องจ่ายเงินมัดจำไหม**
	dtô:ng jàai ngurn mát-jam mái?
Can I pay by credit card?	**ฉันใช้เครดิตการ์ดจ่ายได้ ไหม**
	chan chái kree-dit-gáat jàai dâai mái?
What petrol does it take?	**มันใช้น้ำมันประเภทไหน**
	man chái náam-man bpra-pêet näi?

Driving

Driving a car in Bangkok can be difficult; the traffic is bad, especially during the rush hours. For long-distance driving, especially in the southern areas, you should be aware that some of the roads are narrow and you should drive with extra care.

| **ระวัง/อันตราย** | caution/danger |
| ra-wang/an-dta-raai | |

หยุด yùt	stop
ทางด่วน taang dùan	motorway
ใจกลางเมือง jai glaang muang	town centre

Can I park here?	ฉันจอดตรงนี้ได้ไหม chan jòrt dtrong níi dâai mái?
How long can I park for?	ฉันจอดตรงนี้ได้กี่ชั่วโมง chan jòrt dtrong níi dâai gìi chûa-moong?
We are driving to...	เราจะขับไปที่... rao ja kàp bpai tîi...
Is the road good?	สภาพถนนดีไหม sa-paab tà-nön dii mái?
How long will it take?	ใช้เวลากี่ชั่วโมง chái wee-laa gìi chûa-moong?

คุณขับรถเร็วเกินไป khun kàp rót reo gurn bpai	You are driving too fast
ขอดูใบขับขี่ kör duu bai kàp-kìi	Your driving licence, please

Petrol

Petrol is widely available at petrol stations, which are found along most roads.

น้ำมันเบ็นซิน náam man ben-sin	petrol
เบ็นซินไร้สารตะกั่ว ben-sin rái säan ta-gùa	unleaded petrol
ดีเซล dii-sell	diesel

Where is the nearest petrol station?	ปั๊มน้ำมันที่ใกล้ที่สุดอยู่ที่ไหน bpám náam man tîi glâi tîi sut yùu tîi näi?
Fill it up, please	เติมถัง dtem täng
unleaded	เบ็นซินไร้สารตะกั่ว ben-sin rái säan ta-gùa
diesel	ดีเซล dii-sell
Please check the oil	ตรวจน้ำมันด้วย dtrùat náam man dûai

50

| Can I pay by credit card? | ฉันใช้เครดิตการ์ดจ่ายได้ไหม |
| | chan chái kree-dit-gáat jàai dâai mái? |

YOU MAY HEAR...

| เราไม่มี...
rao mâi mii... | We have no... |
| คุณต้องเปลี่ยนน้ำมันเครื่อง/ใส่น้ำ/เติมแอร์
khun dtô:ng bplìan náam man krûang/sài náam/dturm air | You need oil/water/air |

Breakdown

• •

Most of the petrol stations have their own mechanics who are able to help with car problems, should you have any.

| My car has broken down | รถของฉันเสีย
rót kö:ng chan sïa |

Can you help me?	คุณจะช่วยผม/ ดิฉัน ได้ไหม khun ja chûai pöm/ di-chan dâai mái?
I've run out of petrol	รถผม/ดิฉัน น้ำมันหมด rót pöm/di-chan náam man mòd
I have a flat tyre	รถผม/ดิฉัน ยางแบน rót pöm/di-chan yaang baen
Where is the nearest garage? (repair shop)	อู่ซ่อมรถที่ใกล้ที่สุดอยู่ ที่ไหน ùu sô:m rót tîi glâi tîi sut yùu tîi näi?
Can you repair it?	คุณจะซ่อมมันได้ไหม khun ja sô:m man dâai mái?
How long will it take?	ใช้เวลานานเท่าไหร่ chái wee-laa naan tâo rài?
How much will it cost?	จะต้องจ่ายเท่าไหร่ ja dtô:ng jàai tâo rài?

Car parts

• •

...doesn't work	...เสีย ...sĭa

Where is the repair shop?	อู่ซ่อมรถอยู่ที่ไหน	ùu sôːm rót yùu tîi näi?
accelerator	คันเร่ง	kan rêng
alternator	ไดชาร์ต	dai cháat
battery	แบ็ตเตอรี่	baːt-tur-rii
brakes	เบรค	breek
choke	โช้ค	chook
clutch	คลัทช์	klatch
engine	เครื่องยนต์	krûang-yon
exhaust pipe	ท่อไอเสีย	tôr-ai-sìa
fuse	ฟิวส์	fiu
gears	เกียร์	giaa
handbrake	เบรคมือ	breek-mu
headlights	ไฟหน้า	fai-nâa
ignition	ระบบจุดระเบิด	ra-bob-jut-ra-bùrt
ignition key	กุญแจ	gun-jae
indicator	สัญญาณไฟ	sän-yaan-fai
lock	ล็อค	loːck
radiator	หม้อน้ำ	môr náam
reverse gear	เกียร์ถอยหลัง	gia toːy läng

seat belt	เข็มขัดนิรภัย	këm-kat nì-ra-pai
spark plug	หัวเทียน	hüa tian
steering wheel	พวงมาลัย	puang-maa-lai
tyre	ยาง	yaang
wheel	ล้อ	lór
windscreen	กระจกหน้า	gra-jòk-nâa
windscreen wiper	ที่ปัดน้ำฝน	tîi-pat-náam-fön

Road signs

• •

Thai speed limits are in kilometres per hour. Tolls are charged on some motorways.

ห้ามกลับรถ	hâam klàp rót	no U-turn
ทางเข้า	taang kâo	entrance
ทางออก	taang-òrk	exit
ทางด่วน	taang dùan	motorway
ถนน	tà-nön	road
เลี้ยวซ้าย	líao sáai	turn left
เลี้ยวขวา	líao kwäa	turn right

เดินรถทางเดียว	durn rót taang diao	one way
สุดทางใหญ่	sut-taang-yài	major road ends
ห้ามเข้า	hâam kâo	no entry
เหนือ	nüa	north
ใต้	dtâai	south
ตะวันออก	dta-wan-òrk	east
ตะวันตก	dta-wan-dtòk	west
ทางข้ามถนน	taang kâam tà-nön	pedestrian crossing
ใจกลางเมือง	jai glaang muang	city centre
ลดความเร็ว	lod-kwaam reo	reduce speed
ห้ามทำเสียงรบกวน	hâam tam sïang róp-guan	no sounding of horn
หยุด	yùt	stop
อันตราย	an-dta-raai	danger
โรงพยาบาล	roong-pa-yaa-baan	hospital
ห้ามจอด	hâam jòrt	no parking
ที่จอด	tîi jòrt	parking

Staying somewhere

Hotel (booking)

Hotels are rated in stars from 1 to 5. Big cities such as Bangkok, Phuket and Chiang Mai also have guesthouses and bed and breakfasts.

โรงแรม roong-raem	hotel
เกสท์เฮาส์/ ห้องเช่าพร้อม อาหารเช้า guesthouse/hô:ng-châo pró:m aa-häan cháo	guesthouse/ bed and breakfast
ว่าง/ไม่ว่าง wâang/mâi wâang	vacancies/ no vacancies

A เราต้องการจอง ห้องเดี่ยว/ห้องคู่ หนึ่งห้อง
rao dtôːng gaan jorng hôːng-dìao/hôːng-kûu nùng hôːng
We would like to book a single/double room

B จองกี่คืน
joːng gìi kuun?
For how many nights?

A หนึ่งคืน/สองคืน/หนึ่งอาทิตย์
nùng kuun/sǒːng kuun/nùng aa-tít
for one night/two nights/one week

Is there a hotel/ guesthouse nearby?	ใกล้ใกล้นี้มีโรงแรมหรือ เกสท์เฮาส์ไหม glâi glâi níi mii roong-raem rǔu guesthouse mái?
Do you have a room?	มีห้องว่างไหม mii hôːng wâang mái?
I'd like...	ฉันต้องการ… chan dtôːng gaan...
a single room	ห้องเดี่ยว hôːng dìao
a double room	ห้องคู่ hôːng kûu

57

a room for 3 people	ห้องสำหรับสามคน
	hô:ng säm-ràp säam kon
with shower	พร้อมฝักบัว
	prórm fàk-bua
with bath	พร้อมอ่างอาบน้ำ
	prórm àang àap náam
How much is it per night?	ต่อคืนราคาเท่าไหร่
	dtòr kuun raa-kaa tâo rài?
Is breakfast included?	รวมอาหารเช้าไหม
	ruam aa-häan cháao mái?
I'll be staying...	ฉันจะอยู่...
	chan ja yùu...
We'll be staying...	เราจะอยู่...
	rao ja yùu...
1 night	หนึ่งคืน
	nùng kuun
2 nights	สองคืน
	sö:ng kuun
3 nights	สามคืน
	säam kuun
Is there anywhere else to stay?	มีที่พักที่อื่นอีกบ้างไหม
	mii tîi-pák tîi ùun ìik bâang mái?

YOU MAY HEAR...

กรุณาบอกชื่อของคุณ ka-ru-naa bò:k chûu kŏng khun	Your name, please
ขอดูหนังสือเดินทาง kŏr duu năng-sŭu-dun-taang	Your passport, please
ห้องเต็ม hô:ng dtem	We are full

Hotel (desk)

I have a reservation	**ฉันจองห้องไว้** chan jo:ng hô:ng wái
My name is...	**ฉันชื่อ…** chan chûu...
Have you a different room?	**มีห้องอื่นอีกไหม** mii hô:ng ùun ìik mái?
Where can I park the car?	**ฉันจะจอดรถได้ที่ไหน** chan ja jòrt rót dâai tîi näi?
What time is breakfast?	**อาหารเช้าเสริฟกี่โมง** aa-häan cháao surp gìi moong?

What time is dinner?	อาหารเย็นเสริฟกี่โมง
	aa-häan yen surp gìi moong?
The key, please	ขอกุญแจ
	kör gun-jae
Room number...	ห้องเบอร์...
	hô:ng bur...
Are there any messages for me?	มีข้อความถึงฉันหรือไม่
	mii kôr-kwaam tüng chan rüu mâi?
I'm leaving tomorrow	ฉันจะออกพรุ่งนี้
	chan ja òrk prûng-nii
Please prepare the bill	กรุณาเตรียมบิลไว้ด้วย
	ga-ru-naa dtriam bill wái dûoy
I'd like an early morning call at 7 am.	ฉันต้องการบริการปลุกเจ็ดโมงเช้า
	chan dtô:ng gaan bo-ri-gaan bplùk jèt moong cháao

Shopping

Shopping phrases

••

Shopping centres in Bangkok and other big cities are open from 10.00 am to 9.00 pm Monday to Sunday. In most of the shops it is possible to negotiate the price with the seller.

FACE TO FACE

A ฉันต้องการซื้อชุดสีฟ้า
chan dtô:ng gaan súu chùt-síi-fáa
I would like to buy a blue dress

B คุณใส่ขนาดอะไร
khun sài kà-nàat à-rai?
What is your size?

A ขนาด 34/32
kà-nàat säam sìp sìi/säam sìp sö:ng
size 34/32

Where are the shops?	ร้านค้าอยู่ที่ไหน
	ráan káa yùu tîi näi?
I'm looking for...	ฉันมองหา...
	chan morng häa...
Where is the nearest...?	...ที่ใกล้ที่สุดอยู่ไหน
	...tîi glâi tîi sut yùu tîi näi?
Where is the nearest baker's?	ร้านขนมปังที่ใกล้ที่สุดอยู่ไหน
	ráan ka-nöm bpang tîi glâi tîi sut yùu tîi näi?
Where is the bazaar?	ตลาดนัดอยู่ที่ไหน
	dtà-làat nat yùu tîi näi?
Is it open?	มันเปิดไหม
	man bpùrt mái?
When does it close?	มันปิดเมื่อไหร่
	man bpìt mûa rai?
Can I take that one?	ฉันซื้ออันนี้ได้ไหม
	chan súu an níi dâai mái?
How much is it?	ราคาเท่าไหร่
	raa-kaa tâo rài?
It's too expensive	มันแพงเกินไป
	man paeng gurn bpai
I don't want it	ฉันไม่ต้องการมัน
	chan mâi dtô:ng gaan man

Shops

Where is...?	...อยู่ที่ไหน	
	...yùu tîi näi?	
Where is the baker's?	ร้านขนมปังอยู่ที่ไหน	
	ráan ka-nöm bpang yùu tîi näi?	
baker's	ร้านขนมปัง	ráan ka-nöm bpang
bookshop	ร้านหนังสือ	ráan näng-süü
butcher's	ร้านขายเนื้อสัตว์	ráan käai nûa-sàt
cake shop	ร้านเค้ก	ráan kéek
clothes shop	ร้านเสื้อผ้า	ráan sûa-pâa
electrical goods	ร้านเครื่องไฟฟ้า	ráan krûang fai-fáa
fishmonger's	ร้านขายปลา	ráan käai bplaa
furniture shop	ร้านเฟอร์นิเจอร์	ráan fur-ni-jur
gifts/ souvenirs	ร้านของที่ระลึก	ráan kö:ng tîi ra-lúk
greengrocer's	ร้านขายผัก	ráan käai pàk
grocer's	ร้านขายของชำ	ráan käai kö:ng cham

hairdresser's	ร้านตัดผม	ráan dtat pŏm
jeweller's	ร้านเครื่องเพชร	ráan krûang pét
market	ตลาด	dta-làat
newsagent	ร้านหนังสือพิมพ์	ráan năng-sŭu pim
optician	ร้านแว่นตา	ráan wâen-dtaa
pharmacy	ร้านขายยา	ráan kăai yaa
shoe shop	ร้านรองเท้า	ráan ro:ng táao
shop	ร้านค้า	ráan káa
shopping centre	ห้างสรรพสินค้า	hâang sàp-pa-sĭn-káa
spice/herb shop	ร้านเครื่องเทศ	ráan krûang-têet
stationer's	ร้านเครื่องเขียน	ráan krûang kĭan
supermarket	ซุปเปอร์มาร์เก็ต	sup-bpur-maa-gét
tobacconist's	ร้านบุหรี่	ráan bu-rìi
toy shop	ร้านของเล่น	ráan kŏ:ng lên

Food (general)

bread	ขนมปัง	ka-nöm bpang
butter	เนย	neei
cakes	เค็ก	kéek
cheese	ชีส	chiis
chicken	ไก่	gài
chocolate	ช็อกโกแล็ต	chock-goo-laet
coffee (instant)	กาแฟ	gaa-fae
coffee	กาแฟเม็ด	gaa-fae-met
crisps	มันฝรั่งทอด	man-fa-ràng- tôrt
egg	ไข่	kài
fish	ปลา	bplaa
flour	แป้ง	bpâeng
honey	น้ำผึ้ง	náam-pûng
jam	แยม	yaem
margarine	เนยเทียม	neei-tiam
marmalade	แยมผลไม้	yaem pönla-máai
milk	นม	nom
olive oil	น้ำมันมะกอก	náam-man ma-gòrk
orange juice	น้ำส้ม	náam sôm

pasta	พาสต้า	pass-tâa
pepper (seasoning)	พริกไทย	prik-tai
rice	ข้าว	kâao
salt	เกลือ	glua
stock cubes	ก้อนปรุงน้ำแกง	kô:n-bprung-náam-gaeng
sugar	น้ำตาล	náam-dtaan
tea	ชา	chaa
vinegar	น้ำส้มสายชู	náam-sôm-säai-shuu
yoghurt	โยเกิตร์	yoo-gurt

Food (fruit and veg)

Fruit

apples	แอ๊ปเบิ้ล	ab-bpûrn
bananas	กล้วย	glûai
cherries	เชอรี่	chur-rii
durian	ทุเรียน	tú-rian

grapes	องุ่น	a-ngùn
lime	มะนาว	ma-nauw
longan	ลำไย	lam-yai
mango	มะม่วง	má-mûang
mangosteen	มังคุด	mang-kút
melon	แตงเขียว	dtaeng-kiao
nectarines	ลูกท้อ	lûuk-tór
oranges	ส้ม	sôm
peaches	พีช	peach
pears	แพร์	pear
pineapple	สับปะรด	sap-bpa-rod
plums	พลัม	plam
pomegranate	ทับทิม	tâb-tim
rambutan	เงาะ	ngó:
strawberries	สตรอเบอรี่	sa-dtror-bur-rii
watermelon	แตงโม	dtaeng-moo

Vegetables

cabbage	กะหล่ำปลี	ga-làm-bplii
carrots	แครอท	kae-rò:t
cauliflower	ดอกกะหล่ำ	dorg-ka-làm

English	Thai	Transliteration
cucumber	แตงกวา	dtaeng-gwaa
garlic	กระเทียม	gra- tiam
green beans	ถั่วเขียว	tùa-kïao
lettuce	ผักกาดแก้ว	pàk-gaad-gâew
mushrooms	เห็ด	hèt
onions	หอมใหญ่	hörm-yai
peas	ถั่ว	tùa
peppers	พริกไทย	prik-tai
potatoes	มันฝรั่ง	man-fa-ràng
spinach	ผักโขม	pàk-köom
tomatoes	มะเขือเทศ	má-küa-têet

Clothes

women's sizes		men's suit sizes		shoe sizes			
UK	TH	UK	EU	UK	TH	UK	TH
10	9	36	36	2	5	7	10
12	11	38	38	3	6	8	11
14	13	40	40	4	7	9	12
16	15	42	42	5	8	10	13
18	17	44	44	6	9	11	14
20	19	46	46				

A ฉันลองตัวนี้ได้ไหม

chan lorng dtua níi dâai mái?

Can I try this one on?

B ได้ครับ/ค่ะ ที่ห้องนี้ครับ/ค่ะ

dâai krab/ká tîi hô:ng níi krab/ká

Yes, of course, you can try it on in here

A มีขนาดเล็ก/กลาง/ใหญ่ ไหมครับ/คะ

mii kà-nàat lék/glaang/yài mái krab/ká?

Is there a small/medium/large size for this one?

B มีครับ/ค่ะ/ไม่มีครับ/ค่ะ

mii krab/ká/mâi mii krab/ká

Yes, there is/no, there isn't

Is it real leather?	หนังแท้ไหม
	năng táe mái?
Do you have this one in other colours?	อันนี้มีสีอื่นไหม
	an-níi mii sĭi ùun mái?
It's too expensive	มันแพงเกินไป
	man paeng gurn bpai
It's too big	มันใหญ่เกินไป
	man yài gurnn bpai

69

It's too small	มันเล็กเกินไป
	man lék gurn bpai
No thanks, I don't want it	ไม่เอา ขอบคุณ ฉันไม่ต้องการมัน
	mâi ao kòrb-kun chan mâi dtô:ng gaan man

Clothes (articles)

cotton	ผ้าฝ้าย	pâa-fâai
leather	หนัง	näng
silk	ผ้าไหม	pâa-mäi
wool	ขนสัตว์	kön-sàt
coat	เสื้อคลุม	sûa-klum
dress	กระโปรงชุด	gra-bproong-shút
hat	หมวก	mùak
jacket	เสื้อเจ็กเก็ต	sûa-jack-gét
knickers	กางเกงใน ผู้หญิง	gaang-geng-nai-pûu-yïng
sandals	รองเท้าแตะ	ro:ng-táo-dtà:
shirt	เสื้อ	sûa

> **Paying** (p 97)

shorts	กางเกงขาสั้น	gaang-geng-käa-sân
skirt	กระโปรง	gra-bproong
socks	ถุงเท้า	tüng-táo
swimsuit	ชุดว่ายน้ำ	shút-wâai-náam
t-shirt	เสื้อยืด	sûa-yûud
trousers	กางเกงขายาว	gaang-geng-käa-yao
underpants	กางเกงใน	gaang-geng-nai

Maps and guides

●●●●●●●●●●●●●●●●●●●●●●●●●●●●●●●●●●●●●●●

You can get a free copy of a map of Thailand and
some big-city maps at the TAT (Tourism Authority of
Thailand) counter at the airport. Some big hotels
also provide free city maps for their customers.

Where can I buy a map?	ฉันจะซื้อแผนที่ได้ที่ไหน
	chan ja súu päen-tîi dâai tîi näi?
Do you have a road map?	คุณมีแผนที่ของถนนไหม
	khun mii päen-tîi kö:ng tà-nön mái?
Do you have a town plan?	คุณมีผังเมืองไหม
	khun mii päng muang mái?

Do you have a leaflet/ guidebook in English?	คุณมีคู่มือแนะนำการท่อง เที่ยวไหม
	khun mii kûu-muu naé-nam gaan tô:ng-tîao mái?
Can you show me where … is on the map?	คุณช่วยบอกผม/ดิฉัน หน่อยว่า … อยู่ตรงไหนบนแผนที่
	khun chûai bòrk pöm/di-chan nò:i wâa … yùu dtrong näi bon päen-tîi?
Where can I buy a newspaper?	ฉันจะซื้อหนังสือพิมพ์ได้ที่ ไหน
	chan ja súu näng-süu pim dâai tîi näi?
Have you any English newspapers?	คุณมีหนังสือพิมพ์ภาษา อังกฤษไหม
	khun mii näng-süu pim paa-säa ang-grìt mái?

> **Asking the way** (p 30)
> **Sightseeing and tourist office** (p 76)

Post office

Post offices which are run by the government are open from 8.30 am to 3.30 pm, Monday to Friday. Some big hotels offer mailing services which cost a little more. There are also some other private companies such as FedEx and UPS which offer faster services, and have longer business hours.

ทางอากาศ taang- aa- gàat	airmail
ต่างประเทศ dtàang bpra têet	overseas
ในประเทศ nai bpra-têet	inland
ในพื้นที่ nai púun-tîi	local
จดหมาย jòt- mäai	letter
ไปรษณียบัตร prai-sa-nii-ya-bàt	postcard
แสตมป์ sà-dtaem	stamps

Where is the post office?	ไปรษณีย์อยู่ที่ไหน bprai-sa-nii yùu tîi näi?
Where can I buy stamps?	ฉันจะซื้อแสตมป์ได้ที่ไหน chan ja súu sà-dtaem dâai tîi näi?
5 stamps	แสตมป์ห้าดวง sà-dtaem hâa duang
10 stamps	แสตมป์สิบดวง sà-dtaem sìp duang
for postcards	สำหรับไปรษณียบัตร säm-räp prai-sa-nii-ya-bàt
for letters	สำหรับจดหมาย säm-räp jòt-mäai
to Britain	ส่งไปอังกฤษ sòng bpai ang-grit
to America	ส่งไปอเมริกา sòng bpai a-may-ri-gaa
to Australia	ส่งไปออสเตรเลีย sòng bpai o:s-dtray-lia

> **Money** (p 96) > **Paying** (p 97)

Photos

Where is a photographic shop?	ร้านถ่ายภาพอยู่ที่ไหน ráan tàai-pâap yùu tîi nǎi?
I need a film for this camera	ฉันต้องการฟิลม์สีสำหรับกล้องถ่ายรูปอันนี้ chan dtô:ng-gaan film sǐi säm-räp klô:ng tàai ruub an níi
I need batteries for this	ฉันต้องการแบ็ตเตอรี่สำหรับสิ่งนี้ chan dtô:ng-gaan baet-dtur-rì säm-räp sìng níi
I'd like these films developed	ฉันต้องการล้างรูปและอัดภาพ chan dtô:ng-gaan láang ruub laé àt pâap
How long will it take?	จะใช้เวลานานเท่าไหร่ ja chái wee-laa naan tâo rài?
How much will it cost?	ราคาเท่าไหร่ raa-kaa tâo rài?

Leisure

Sightseeing and tourist office

Tourist offices provide lists of accommodation, maps and leaflets describing local attractions.

Thai		English
ข้อมูล	kôr-moon	information
สำนักงานการท่องเที่ยว säm-nak-ngaan-gaan- tô:ng tîao		tourist office
พิพิธภัณฑ์	pí-pít-ta-pan	museum
ห้องแสดงศิลปะ hô:ng sa-daeng sín-lá-bpà		art gallery
วัด	wát	temple
ทัวร์นำเที่ยว tuaa-nam-tîao		guided tour

ตั๋ว dtŭa	tickets
ห้องสุขา hôːng su-kăa	toilet

Where is the tourist office?	สำนักงานการท่องเที่ยวอยู่ที่ไหน
	säm-nak-ngaan-gaan- tôːng tîao yùu tîi näi?
What can we visit in the area?	บริเวณนั้นมีอะไรบ้าง
	boː-ri-ween nán mii a-rai bâang?
Have you got details in English?	มีรายละเอียดเป็นภาษาอังกฤษไหม
	mii raai là-ìat bpen paa-säa ang-grìt mái?
Are there any excursions?	มีโปรแกรมเที่ยวระยะสั้นไหม
	mii bpro-graem tîao rá-yá sân mái?
When does it leave?	จะไปเมื่อไหร่
	ja bpai mûa-rai?
When does it get back?	จะกลับเมื่อไหร่
	ja glàb mûa-rai?

> **Maps and guides** (p 71)

Entertainment

What is there to do in the evenings?	มีอะไรที่น่าทำตอนเย็นบาง
	mii à-rai tîi nâa tam dto:n yen bâang?
We would like to go to a disco	เราต้องการไปเธค
	rao dtông gaan bpai tek
Is there anywhere we can go to hear live music?	ที่ไหนมีการแสดงดนตรีสดบาง
	tîi näi mii gaan sa-daeng don-dtrii sòt bâang?
Is there anywhere we can go to see Thai dancing?	ที่ไหนมีการแสดงรำไทยบาง
	tîi näi mii gaan-sa-daeng ram-tai bâang?
Is there any entertainment for children?	ที่ไหนมีความบันเทิงสำหรับเด็ก
	tîi näi mii kwaam ban-turng säm-räp dèk?

Leisure/beach

ชายหาด	chaai-hàat	**beach**
อันตราย	an-dta-raai	**danger**
ฝักบัว	fàk bua	**showers**

Are there any good beaches round here?
แถวนี้มีหาดสวย สวย บ้างไหม
täew níi mii hàat süai süai bâang mái?

Is there a bus (shared taxi) to the beach?
มีรถบัส (รถประจำทาง) ไปชายหาดไหม
mii rót bás (rót-bpra-jam-taang) bpai chaai-hàat mái?

Can we go windsurfing?
เราเล่นกระดานโต้คลื่น ได้ไหม
rao lên grà daan dtôo klûun dâai mái?

Please go away!
กรุณาอย่ารบกวนครับ/ค่ะ
ga-ru-naa yàa róp-guan krab/kà!

> **Sport** (p 85) > **Walking** (p 86)

Music

Is there anywhere we can go to hear music?
เราจะไปฟังเพลงได้ที่ไหนบ้าง
rao ja bpai fang pleeng dâai tîi näi bâang?

Are there any concerts?
ที่ไหนมีคอนเสิร์ตบ้าง
tîi näi mii ko:n-surt bâang?

Where can I get tickets?
ฉันจะซื้อตั๋วได้ที่ไหนบ้าง
chan ja súu dtüa dâai tîi näi bâang?

Where can I hear some classical music/jazz?
ฉันจะไปฟังเพลงคลาสสิก/เพลงแจ๊สได้ที่ไหนบ้าง
chan ja bpai fang pleeng clas-sic/ jass dâai tîi näi bâang?

Cinema

โรงหนัง	roong-näng	cinema
ฉาย	chäai	screening

> **Making friends** (p 24)

What's on at the cinema?	มีหนังอะไรฉายบ้าง
	mii näng à-rai chäai bâang?
What time does the film start?	หนังฉายกี่โมง
	näng chäai gìi moong?
How much are the tickets?	ตั๋วหนังราคาเท่าไหร่
	dtüa näng raa-kaa tâo rài?
Two for (give name and time of performance) showing	ตั๋วสองใบเรื่อง…
	dtüa sö:ng bai rûang...

YOU MAY HEAR...

หนังเรื่อง ... ตั๋วหมดแล้วครับ/ค่ะ	For screening ... we have no tickets left
näng rûang ... dtüa mòt láew krab/ká	

Temple

Dress appropriately when you go to the temples. Never wear sleeveless tops, shorts or short skirts, as you will not be allowed in. Shoes have to be taken off once inside the chapel where the principal image of Buddha is kept. Do not climb onto the

81

Buddha image to take a photograph or do anything that may indicate a lack of respect.

Buddhist monks are forbidden to touch or be touched by a woman. If a woman has to give anything to a monk, she should ask a man to pass it to the monk. If there is not a man around, the monk will put a cloth on a table, and then the woman can place the item on the cloth.

Thai	English
วัด wát	temple
ศาสนาพุทธ sàat-sà-nǎa-put	Buddhist
ศาสนาคริสต์ sàat-sà-nǎa-kris	Christian
รองเท้า ro:ng-táao	shoes
ห้ามถ่ายภาพ hâam tàai-pâap	no photos
ห้ามถ่ายวิดีโอ hâam tàai video	no videos

English	Thai
I'd like to see the temple	ฉันต้องการไปดูวัด chan dtô:ng gaan bpai duu wát

When can we see the temple?	เมื่อไหร่เราจะได้ไปวัด
	mûa-rai rao ja dâai bpai wát?
Where is the temple?	วัดอยู่ที่ไหน
	wát yùu tîi näi?

Television

The state channel TRT3 has the news in English, German and French and some films with original language subtitles. Most of the hotels and bars have a satellite dish.

รีโมทคอนโทรล rii mòot ko:n trool	remote control
ข่าว kàao	news
เปิดทีวี bpùrd tii-vii	to switch on
ปิดทีวี bpìd tii-vii	to switch off
การ์ตูน gaar-tuun	cartoons

Where is the television?	โทรทัศน์อยู่ไหน
	too-rà-tát yùu näi?
How do I switch on the television?	ฉันจะเปิดทีวีได้อย่างไร
	chan ja bpùrd tii-vii dâai yàang rai?
What's on television?	มีรายการทีวีอะไรบ้าง
	mii raai-gaan tii-vii a-rai bâang?
Are there any English-speaking channels?	มีช่องไหนที่เป็นภาษา อังกฤษบ้าง
	mii chô:ng näi tîi bpen paa-säa ang-grìt bâang?
Are there any children's programmes?	มีช่องไหนที่มีรายการเด็ก บาง
	mii ch ô:ng näi tîi mii raai-gaan dèk bâang?
When is the football/news on?	เมื่อไหร่จะมีรายการ ฟุตบอล/รายการข่าว
	mûa-rai ja mii raai-gaan fut-bo:n/ raai-gaan kàao?

Sport

Where can we play tennis/golf/football?
เราจะไปเล่นเทนนิส/กอล์ฟ/ฟุตบอล ได้ที่ไหน
rao ja bpai lên ten-nïs/go:f/ fut-bo:n dâai tïi näi?

Can we play tennis/golf?
เราเล่นเทนนิส/กอลฟ์ ได้ไหม
rao lên ten-nïs/go:f dâai mái?

Can we hire rackets/golf clubs?
เราเช่าไม้เทนนิส/ไมกอลฟ์ ได้ไหม
rao châo mái ten-nïs/ mái go:f dâai mái?

How much is it per hour?
ชั่วโมงละเท่าไหร่
chûa-moong lá tâo-rài?

Can we watch a football match?
ให้เราดูรายการฟุตบอล ไดไหม
hâi rao duu raai-gaan fut-bo:n dâai mái?

Where can we get tickets?
เราจะซื้อตั๋วได้ที่ไหน
rao ja súu dtüa dâai tïi näi?

85

How do we get to the stadium?

เราจะไปสนามกีฬาได้
อย่างไร

rao ja bpai sà-näam gii-laa dâai
yàang-rai?

Walking

Are there any guided walks?

มีทัวร์นำเดินเที่ยวไหม

mii tuaa nam durn-tîaw mái?

Do you have a guide to local walks?

คุณมีคู่มือเดินเที่ยวใน
พื้นที่ไหม

khun mii kûu-muu durn-tîaw nai
púun-tîi mái?

How many kilometres is the walk?

ระยะทางเดินกี่กิโลเมตร

rá-yá taang durn gìi gi-loo-met?

How long will it take?

ใช้เวลานานเท่าไหร่

chái wee-laa naan tâo rài?

Is it very steep?

ทางชันมากไหม

taang chan mâak mái?

I'd like to go climbing

ฉันต้องการไปปีนเขา

chan dtô:ng gaan bpai bpiin käo

> **Maps and guides** (p 71)

Leisure

Communications

Telephone and mobile

A phonecard is the most convenient way to make an international call. To call from Thailand to the UK dial **00**, and then **44**, followed by the area code. To call from the UK to Thailand dial **00**, and then **66**, followed by the area code. For example, Bangkok's area code is **2**, so you dial **00-662-phone number**. Call **1313** for the phone directory.

เหรียญโทรศัพท์ rĭan too-rá-sàp	phone token
บัตรโทรศัพท์ bàt too-rá-sàp	phonecard
หนังสือโทรศัพท์ năng-sǔu too-rá-sàp	telephone directory
เก็บเงินปลายทาง gèb ngurn bplaai taang	reverse charges (collect)

รหัสโทรศัพท์	dialling code
rà-hàt too-rá-sàp	

Hello, I am...

สวัสดีครับ/ค่ะ ผม/ดิฉัน...
sa-wad-dii krab/ka pöm/
di-chan...

I would like to
speak to...

**ผม/ดิฉัน
ต้องการพูดกับคุณ...**
pöm/di-chan dtô:ng gaan pûud
gàb khun...

I want to make
a phone call

ฉันต้องการใช้โทรศัพท์
chan dtô:ng gaan chái too-rá-sàp

I want to phone
the UK

ฉันต้องการโทรฯไปอังกฤษ
chan dtô:ng gaan too bpai ang-grìt

An outside line,
please

ต่อสายนอกครับ/ค่ะ
dtòr säai nôrk krab/ka

Where can I buy
a phonecard?

**ฉันจะซื้อบัตรโทรศัพท์ได้
ที่ไหน**
chan ja súu bàt too-rá-sàp dâai tíi
näi?

Please write the
phone number
down

กรุณาจดเบอร์โทรศัพท์
ga-ru-naa jòd bur too-rá-sàp

Do you have a mobile phone?	คุณมีโทรศัพท์มือถือไหม
	khun mii too-rá-sàp muu tüu mái?
Can I speak to...	ฉันต้องการพูดกับ...
	chan dtô:ng gaan puud kàb...
This is...	นี้คือ...
	níi kuu...
I'll call back later	ฉันจะโทรฯกลับมาใหม่
	chan ja too klàb maa mài
I'll call again tomorrow	ฉันจะโทรฯมาใหม่พรุ่งนี้
	chan ja too maa mài prûng níi

YOU MAY HEAR...	
สวัสดีครับ/ค่ะ sa-wad-dii krab/kà	Hello
กรุณาถือสายรอสักครู่ ga-ru-naa tüu säai ror sak-krûu	Please hold on
ใครโทรฯมา krai too maa?	Who is calling?
คุณโทรฯกลับมาใหม่ได้ไหมครับ/คะ khun too glàb maa mài dâai mái krab/kà?	Can you call back later?

| คุณต้องการทิ้ง ข้อความไว้ไหม
khun dtô:ng gaan tíng kôr-kwaam wâi mái? | Do you want to leave a message? |
| คุณโทรฯเบอร์ผิด
khun too bur pìd | Wrong number |

Text messaging

SMS has become popular in Thailand.

I will text you	ฉันจะส่งข้อความถึงคุณ chan ja sòng kôr-kwaam tüng khun
Can you text me?	คุณจะส่งข้อความถึงฉัน ได้ไหม khun ja sòng kôr-kwaam tüng chan dâai mái?
Did you get my text message?	คุณได้รับข้อความของฉัน ไหม khun dâai ráb kôr-kwaam kö:ng chan mái?

Can you send me a picture from your mobile?	คุณสามารถส่งรูปจากโทรศัพท์มือถือของคุณได้หรือไม่
	khun säa-mâat sòng rûub jàak too-rá-sàp muu tüu kö:ng khun dâai rüu mâi?
Hello	สวัสดีครับ/ค่ะ
	sa-wad-dii krab/kà
Hello (to answer the phone)	สวัสดีครับ/ค่ะ
	sa-wad-dii krab/kà
See you	แล้วเจอกัน
	láew jur gan
tomorrow	พรุ่งนี้
	prûng níi
please call me	กรุณาโทรถึงผม/ดิฉัน
	ga-ru-naa too tüng pöm/di-chan
today	วันนี้
	wan níi
too late	สายเกินไป
	säai gurn bpai
tonight	คืนนี้
	kuun níi
text me	ส่งข้อความถึงฉัน
	sòng kôr-kwaam tüng chan

Free to talk?	ว่างที่จะคุยไหม
	wâang tîi ja kui mái?
I'll call you back later	ฉันจะโทรฯถึงคุณทีหลัง
	chan ja too tüng khun tii läng
Thanks	ขอบคุณ
	kòrb kun
Are you OK?	เป็นอะไรหรือเปล่า
	bpen a-rai rüu bplàao?

E-mail

The TLD (internet suffix) for Thailand is **.co.th**

Do you have e-mail?	คุณมีอีเมล์ไหม
	khun mii e-mail mái?
My e-mail address is...	อีเมล์ของฉัน…
	e-mail kö:ng chan...
What is your e-mail address?	อะไรคืออีเมล์ของคุณ
	a-rai kuu e-mail kö:ng khun?
How do you spell it?	สะกดยังไง
	sà-gòt yang ngai?
All one word	เขียนติดกันหมด
	kïan dtìd gan mòt

All lower case	เขียนตัวเล็กหมด
	kïan dtua lék mòt
Can I send an e-mail?	ฉันจะส่งอีเมล์ได้ไหม
	chan ja sòng e-mail dâai mái?
Did you get my e-mail?	คุณได้รับอีเมล์ของฉันไหม
	khun dâai ráb e-mail kö:ng chan mái?

Internet

· ·

It is easy to find an Internet café in Bangkok. In other cities, you will find an Internet service in the big hotels.

โฮมเพจ hoom-pèij	home
ชื่อผู้ใช้ chûu pûu chái	username
ค้นหา kón-häa	to browse
เครื่องค้นหา krûang kón-häa	search engine
รหัส rá-hàt	password
ติดต่อเรา dtìd-dtòr rao	contact us

กลับไปที่รายการเลือก klàb bpai tîi raai-gaan lûak	back to menu
แผนที่เว็บไซต์ päen-tîi web site	sitemap

Are there any Internet cafés here?	มีอินเตอร์เน็ตคาเฟ่ที่ไหนบาง mii in-ter-net kaa-fè tîi näi bâang?
How much is it to log on for an hour?	ค่าบริการชั่วโมงละเท่าไหร่ kâa bo:-ri-gaan chûa-moong lá tâo rài?
I would like to print some pages	ฉันต้องการจะพิมพ์บางหนา chan dtô:ng gaan ja pìm baang nâa

Fax

● ●

You can find fax services at hotels. In the big cities, you also can find fax services at travel agencies.

Addressing a fax

จาก	jàak	from
ถึง	tŭng	to
วันที่	wan-tîi	date
…หน้ารวมทั้งหน้านี้		…pages including this
…nâa ruam-táng nâa níi		one

I want to send a fax	ฉันต้องการส่งแฟกซ์ chan dtô:ng gaan sòng fax
Do you have a fax?	คุณมีแฟกซ์ไหม khun mii fax mái?
Where can I send a fax?	ฉันจะส่งแฟกซ์ได้ที่ไหน chan ja sòng fax dâai tîi nǎi?
How much is it to send a fax?	ค่าส่งแฟกซ์เท่าไหร่ kâa sòng fax tâo rài?
What is your fax number?	แฟกซ์ของคุณหมายเลข อะไร fax kö:ng khun mǎai-lêek a-rai?
The fax number is...	หมายเลขแฟกซ์… mǎai-lêek fax…

Practicalities

Money

● ●

Banking hours are 8.30 am to 3.00 pm, Monday to Friday. Some branches located in shopping centres have longer business hours, some being open from 10.00 am to 9.00 pm. The Thai currency is the **Baht**.

Where is the nearest bank?	ธนาคารที่ใกล้ที่สุดอยู่ที่ไหน ta-naa-kaan tîi glâi tîi-sùt yùu tîi näi?
Where is the nearest currency office?	ที่รับแลกเงินที่ใกล้ที่สุดอยู่ที่ไหน tîi ráb lâek-ngurn tîi glâi tîi-sùt yùu tîi näi?
Can I change money here?	ฉันแลกเงินที่นี่ได้ไหม chan lâek ngurn tîi nîi dâai mái?
What is the exchange rate?	อัตราแลกเปลี่ยนเท่าไหร่ àt-dtraa lâek bplìan tâo rài?

I want to change £50	ฉันต้องการแลก ห้าสิบ ปอนด์
	chan dtô:ng gaan lâek hâa-sìp bporn
I want to buy traveller's cheques (only at banks)	ฉันต้องการซื้อเช็ค เดินทาง
	chan dtô:ng gaan súu check durn-taang

Paying

Credit card payments are accepted; however, a 3% handling fee is added for using them. Service charge in restaurants, bars and cafés is included in the bill.

Thai	English
ใบเก็บเงิน bai- gèb ngurn	bill
ใบเสร็จ bai-sèt	receipt
ใบส่งของ bai- sòng-kö:ng	invoice
โต๊ะเก็บเงิน dtó- gèb ngurn	cash desk
เครดิตการ์ด krei-dit-gáat	credit card

I'd like to pay now	ฉันต้องการจ่ายเงิน
	chan dtô:ng gaan jàai ngurn
How much is it?	ทั้งหมดเท่าไหร่
	táng mòt tâo rài?
Can I pay...?	ฉันใช้ ... จ่ายได้ไหม
	chan chái ... jàai dâai mái?
Can I pay by credit card/cheque?	ฉันใช้เครดิตการ์ด/ เช็คจ่ายได้ไหม
	chan chái kree-dit-gáat/ check jàai dâai mái?
by credit card	ใช้เครดิตการ์ดจ่าย
	chái kree-dit-gáat jàai
with traveller's cheques	ใช้เช็คเดินทางจ่าย
	chái check durn-taang jàai
Where do I pay?	จ่ายเงินที่ไหน
	jàai ngurn tîi näi?
Please write down the price	เขียนราคาให้หน่อย
	kïan raa-kaa hâi nòi
Put it on my bill (in a hotel)	คิดรวมกับค่าที่พักของฉัน
	kìd ruam gàb kâa tîi-pák kö:ng chan
I'd like a receipt, please	ขอใบเสร็จด้วยครับ/ค่ะ
	kör bai-sèt dûoy krab/ká

English	Thai
I think there is a mistake	ฉันคิดว่าคุณคิดตังค์ผิด chan kíd wâa khun kìd dtang pìd
Keep the change	ไม่ต้องคืนเงินทอนครับ/ค่ะ mâi dtô:ng kuun ngurn-torn krab/ká

Luggage

Thai	English
กระเป๋าเดินทาง grà-bpäo-durn-taang	suitcase
กระเป๋าถือ grà-bpäo-tüu	handbag
กระเป๋าเอกสาร grà-bpäo-èek-gà-säan	briefcase
กระเป๋าเดินทางเล็ก grà-bpäo-durn-taang-lék	hand luggage
ที่ติดต่อสัมภาระหาย tîi dtid-dtòr säm-paa-rá häai	left-luggage office
ที่เก็บของ tîi gèb kö:ng	locker
ที่ลากของ tîi lâag kö:ng	trolley

> **Shopping** (p 61)

English	Thai	Transliteration

My suitcase hasn't arrived

กระเป๋าเดินทางของฉันยัง
มาไม่ถึง

grà-bpǎo-durn-taang kö:ng chan
yang maa mâi tüng

My suitcase is missing

กระเป๋าเดินทางของฉัน
หายไป

grà-bpǎo-durn-taang kö:ng chan
häai bpai

My suitcase is damaged

กระเป๋าเดินทางของฉัน
เสียหาย

grà-bpǎo-durn-taang kö:ng chan
sïa häai

Can I leave my suitcase here?

ฉันจะวางกระเป๋าเดินทาง
ตรงนี้ได้ไหม

chan ja waang grà-bpǎo-durn-
taang dtrong níi dâai mái?

Is there a left-luggage office?

ที่ติดต่อสัมภาระหาย
อยู่ไหน

tîi dtid-dtòr säm-paa-rá häai yùu
näi?

When does it open?

มันเปิดเมื่อไหร่

man bpùrd mûa-rài?

When does it close?

มันปิดเมื่อไหร่

man bpìd mûa-rài?

Repairs

ร้านซ่อมรองเท้า ráan sô:m ro:ng-táao	shoe repair shop
ร้านซ่อม รอรับได้ ráan sô:m ror ráb dâai	repairs while you wait

This is broken	อันนี้เสีย an níi sĭa
Where can I get this repaired?	ฉันจะซ่อมอันนี้ได้ที่ไหน chan ja sô:m an níi dâai tîi näi?
Can you repair...?	คุณจะซ่อม ... ได้ไหม khun ja sô:m ... dâai mái?
my glasses?	แว่นตาของฉัน wâen-dtaa kö:ng chan?
my camera?	กล้องถ่ายรูปของฉัน glô:ng tàai ruub kö:ng chan?
How much will it cost?	มันราคาเท่าไหร่ man raa-kaa tâo rài?
How long will it take?	ใช้เวลานานเท่าไหร่ chái wee-laa naan tâo rài?

> **Train** (p 38) > **Air travel** (p 44)

อันนี้ซ่อมไม่ได้ an níi sô:m mâi dâai	I cannot repair this

Laundry

ผงซักฟอก pŏng-sák-fôrk	washing powder
ที่ซักผ้า tîi sák pâa	launderette
บริการซักแห้ง bo:-ri-gaan sák hâeng	dry-cleaner's

Where can I wash some clothes?	**ฉันจะซักเสื้อผ้าได้ที่ไหน** chan ja sák sûa-pâa dâai tîi näi?
Do you have a laundry service?	**คุณมีบริการซักผ้าไหม** khun mii bo:-ri-gaan sák pâa mái?
Where is the launderette?	**ที่ซักผ้าอยู่ที่ไหน** tîi sák pâa yùu tîi näi?
Where is the dry-cleaner's?	**บริการซักแห้งอยู่ที่ไหน** bo:-ri-gaan sák hâeng yùu tîi näi?

> Breakdown (p 51)

| Can I borrow an iron? | ให้ฉันยืมเตารีดได้ไหม |
| | hâi chan yuum dtao-rîid dâai mái? |

YOU MAY HEAR...

| ต่อชิ้น | per item |
| dtòr chín | |

Complaints

This doesn't work	มันไม่ทำงาน
	man mâi tam-ngaan
The room is dirty	ห้องสกปรก
	hô:ng sok-gà-bpròk
The room is too hot	ห้องร้อนเกินไป
	hô:ng rórn gurn bpai
I didn't order this	ฉันไม่ได้สั่งอันนี้
	chan mâi dâai sàng an níi
I want to complain...	ฉันต้องการต่อว่า...
	chan dtô:ng gaan dtòr-wâa...
Please call the manager	กรุณาเรียกผู้จัดการมา
	ga-ru-naa rîak pûu-jàt-gaan maa

Complaints

...out of order	...ปิดซ่อม
	...bbpid sô:m
toilet	ห้องสุขา
	hô:ng su-käa
shower	ห้องอาบน้ำ
	hô:ng àap náam
television	โทรทัศน์
	too-rà-tát

Problems

Can you help me?	คุณจะช่วยฉันได้ไหม
	khun ja chûai chan dâai mái?
I don't speak Thai	ฉันไม่สามารถพูดภาษาไทย
	chan mâi säa-mâat pûud paa-säa thai
Do you speak English?	คุณพูดภาษาอังกฤษได้ไหม
	khun pûud paa-säa ang-grìt dâai mái?

> **Hotel desk** (p 59)

Practicalities

Is there someone who speaks English?	มีใครพูดภาษาอังกฤษได้ไหม
	mii krai pûud paa-säa ang-grìt dâai mái?
I'm lost	ฉันหลงทาง
	chan löng taang
I need to go to...	ฉันต้องการจะไป...
	chan dtô:ng gaan ja bpai...
the station	ที่สถานี
	tîi sà-täa-nii
my hotel	ที่โรงแรม
	tîi roong-raem
this address	ที่อยู่นี้
	tîi yùu níi
I've missed my train/bus/plane	ฉันพลาดรถไฟ/รถเมล์/เครื่องบิน
	chan plâad rót fai/rót meey/ krûang bin
I've missed the connection	ฉันต่อเครื่องไม่ทัน
	chan dtòr krûang mâi tan
The coach has left without me	รถโค้ชออกไปก่อนฉันจะมาถึง
	rót coach òrk bpai gò:n chan ja maa tüng

How does this work?	ทำอย่างไร
	tam yàang-rai?
That man is following me	ผู้ชายคนนั้นตามฉันมา
	pûu-chaai kon nàn dtaam chan maa
I lost my money	ฉันทำเงินหาย
	chan tam ngurn häai

Emergencies

ตำรวจ dtam-rùat	police
ตำรวจดับเพลิง dtam-rùat dàp-plurng	fire brigade
รถพยาบาล rót-pa-yaa-baan	ambulance
โรงพยาบาล roong pa-yaa-baan	hospital

Help!	ช่วยด้วย
	chûai dûoy!
Fire!	ไฟไหม้
	fai mâi!
There's been an accident	มีอุบัติเหตุ
	mii ù-bàt-dtì-hèet
Please help me	กรุณาช่วยฉันด้วย
	ga-ru-naa chûai chan dûoy
Please call the police/fire brigade	ช่วยโทรฯเรียกตำรวจ/ ตำรวจดับเพลิง ด้วย
	chûai too ríak dtam-rùat/ dtam-rùat dàp-plurng dûoy
Someone has been injured	มีคนบาดเจ็บ
	mii kon bàat jèb
Where is the police station?	สถานีตำรวจอยู่ไหน
	sà-täa-nii dtam-rùat yùu näi?
I've been robbed	ฉันถูกปล้น
	chan tùuk bplôn
I've been raped	ฉันถูกข่มขืน
	chan tùuk kòm-küun
I want to speak to a policewoman	ฉันต้องการพูดกับตำรวจผู้ หญิง
	chan dtô:ng gaan pûud gàb dtam-rùat pûu-ying

107

English	Thai
Someone has stolen...	มีคนโขมย... mii kon kà-mooi...
I've lost...	...ของฉันหาย ...kö:ng chan häai
my money	เงินของฉัน ngurn kö:ng chan
my passport	หนังสือเดินทางของฉัน näng-süu-durn-taang kö:ng chan
my plane ticket	ตั๋วเครื่องบินของฉัน dtüa krûang bin kö:ng chan
My son is missing	ลูกชายของฉันหายไป lûuk-chaai kö:ng chan häai bpai
My daughter is missing	ลูกสาวของฉันหายไป lûuk-säao kö:ng chan häai bpai
His/Her name is...	ชื่อของเขา... chûu kö:ng kao...
I need a report for my insurance	ฉันต้องรายงานบริษัทประกัน chan dtô:ng raai-ngaan bò:-ri-sàt bpra-gan
Please call the British Embassy	กรุณาโทรฯไปสถานทูตอังกฤษให้หน่อยครับ/ค่ะ ga-ru-naa too bpai sa-täan-tûut ang-grìt hâi nòi krab/kà

Health

Pharmacy

Pharmacies ร้านขายยา ráan käai yaa are open from 9.00 am to 9.00 pm.

Where is the nearest pharmacy?	ร้านขายยาที่ใกล้ที่สุดอยู่ไหน ráan käai yaa tîi glâi tîi sut yùu näi?
I need something...	ฉันต้องการ... chan dtô:ng gaan...
for diarrhoea	ยาแก้ท้องเสีย yaa gâe tó:ng sïa
for constipation	ท้องผูก ó:ng pùuk
for food poisoning	สำหรับอาหารเป็นพิษ säm-ràp aa-häan bpen pít
Is it safe for...?	มันปลอดภัยสำหรับ ...ไหม man bplòrt pai säm-ràp ... mái?

children	เด็ก
	dèk
I am pregnant	ฉันกำลังท้อง
	chan gamlang tó:ng
What is the dose?	ต้องกินยาอย่างไร
	dtô:ng gin yaa yàang rai?

กินสามครั้งต่อวัน gin säam kráng dtòr wan	3 times a day
ก่อน/หลัง อาหาร gò:n/lang/aa-häan	before/after a meal
กินพร้อมอาหาร gin prórm aa-häan	with a meal

Doctor

โรงพยาบาล roong-pa-ya-baan	hospital
แผนกฉุกเฉิน pà-nàek chùk-chürn	casualty department
ใบสั่งยา bai-sàng-yaa	prescription
รถฉุกเฉิน rót chùk-chürn	ambulance

FACE TO FACE

A **ฉันรู้สึกไม่สบาย**
chan rúu sùk mâi sà baai
I don't feel right

B **คุณมีไข้ไหม**
khun mii kâi mái?
Do you have a temperature?

A **ไม่มี/มี ฉันปวดตรงนี้**
mâi mii/mii chan bpùat dtrong níi
No/Yes, I have a pain here

I have broken...	...ของฉันหัก
	...kö:ng chan hàg
my foot	เท้าของฉัน
	táo kö:ng chan
my ankle	ข้อเท้าของฉัน
	kôr-táo kö:ng chan
my hand	มือของฉัน
	muu kö:ng chan
my arm	แขนของฉัน
	käen kö:ng chan
It hurts	มันเจ็บ
	man jèp
I need to see a doctor	ฉันต้องการไปหาหมอ
	chan dtô:ng gaan bpai häa mör
My son/daughter is ill	ลูกชาย/ลูกสาว ของฉันไม่สบาย
	lûuk chaai/lûuk säao kö:ng chan mâi sà baai
Will he/she have to go to hospital?	ต้องไปโรงพยาบาลไหม
	dtô:ng bpai roong-pa-ya-baan mái?
I'm on the pill	ฉันกำลังกินยาประจำ
	chan gamlang gin yaa bprà jam
I'm diabetic	ฉันเป็นเบาหวาน
	chan bpen bao wäan

I need insulin	ฉันต้องการอินซูลิน
	chan dtô:ng gaan in-suu-lin
I'm allergic to penicillin	ฉันแพ้ยาเพนนิซิลิน
	chan páe yaa pen-ni-si-lin
Will I have to pay?	ฉันต้องจ่ายไหม
	chan dtô:ng jàai mái?
Can you give me a receipt for the insurance?	ขอใบเสร็จสำหรับไปเคลม ประกันด้วยครับ/ค่ะ
	kör bai-sèt säm-ràp bpai claim bpra-gan dûoy krab/ká?

Dentist

You will have to pay for dental treatment at the time of service. Ask for a receipt if you want to claim money back from your insurance company.

อุดฟัน	ùt fan	filling
ครอบฟัน	krôrb fan	crown
ฟันปลอม	fan bplorm	dentures
ฉีดยา	chìid yaa	injection

I need to go to a dentist	ฉันต้องไปหาหมอฟัน
	chan dtôːng bpai hǎa mǒr fan
He/she has toothache	เขา/เธอ ปวดฟัน
	kǎo/tur bpùat fan
This hurts	มันปวด
	man bpùat
My filling has come out	ที่อุดฟันหลุด
	tîi ùt fan lùt
My crown has come out	ที่ครอบฟันหลุด
	tîi krôrb fan lùt
Can you do emergency treatment?	คุณจะสามารถรักษา ได้เลยหรือเปล่า
	khun jà sǎa-mâat rák-sǎa dâai leei rüu bplàao?

Different types of travellers

Disabled travellers

Is there a toilet for the disabled?	มีห้องสุขาสำหรับคนพิการไหม
	mii hô:ng su-käa säm-ràp kon pi-gaan mái?
I want a room on the ground floor	ฉันต้องการห้องชั้นล่าง
	chan dtô:ng gaan hô:ng chán lâang
Can I visit in a wheelchair?	ฉันจะนั่งรถเข็นไปได้ไหม
	chan jà nâng rót-kën bpai dâai mái?
Is there a lift?	ลิฟท์อยู่ที่ไหน
	lift yùu tîi näi?
Is there a reduction for the disabled?	มีส่วนลดให้คนพิการไหม
	mii sùan lód hâi kon pi-gaan mái?
I am deaf	ฉันเป็นคนหูหนวก
	chan bpen kon hüu nùak

> **Hotel (booking)** (p 56) > **Hotel desk** (p 59)

Disabled travellers

With kids

Different types of travellers

A child's ticket	ตั๋วเด็ก
	dtüa dèk
He/she is ... years old	เขา/เธอ อายุ ... ปี
	käo/tur aa-yú ... bpii
Is there a reduction for children?	มีส่วนลดสำหรับเด็กไหม
	mii sùan lód säm-ràp dèk mái?
Do you have a children's menu?	มีรายการอาหารสำหรับ เด็กไหม
	mii raai-gaan aa-häan säm-ràp dèk mái?
Is it OK to take children?	พาเด็กไปด้วยได้ไหม
	paa dèk bpai dûoy dâai mái?
Do you have...?	คุณมี ... ไหม
	khun mii ... mái?
a high chair	โต๊ะสำหรับเด็ก
	dtó säm-ràp dèk
a cot	เปล/เตียงสำหรับเด็ก
	bplee/dtiang säm-ràp dèk

Reference

Alphabet

Thai has 44 consonants and 32 vowel characters. However, there are only 20 consonant sounds. Below are the consonants which are pronounced in the same way as in English.

ก	= **g** as in **g**ood
ข ค ฆ	= **k** as in **k**ing
จ	= **j** as in **J**anuary
ช ส, ษ, ศ	= **s** as in **s**eek
ด, ฎ	= **d** as in **d**oor
บ	= **b** as in **b**aby
ม	= **m** as in **m**other
น ณ	= **n** as in **n**oun
ล ฬ	= **l** as in **l**ove
ร	= **r** as in **r**oll
ว	= **w** as in **w**oman
ท ธ	= **t** as in **t**ime
ย, ญ	= **y** as in **y**ou

ฟ	= **f** as in **f**un
ห ฮ	= **h** as in **h**oney

The following are a few sounds that are difficult to pronounce.

ฏ ด	= **dt** as in s**t**op
ป	= **bp** as in s**p**ain
ช ฌ ฌ	= **ch** as in **ch**ange
ง	= **ng** as in ri**ng**ing

Only 30 of the 32 vowels found in the Thai language are in use. They can be classified in two groups: short vowels and long vowels. The words in this book use a single letter or a single letter followed by a colon for short vowels, and a double letter or a combination of two letters for long vowels ('**a**' for a short vowel, and '**aa**' for a long vowel).

Measurements and quantities

•••••••••••••••••••••••••••••••••

1 lb = approx. 0.5 kilo – 1 pint = approx. 0.5 litre

Liquids

1/2 litre of...	...ครึ่งลิตร	krûng lít
one litre of...	...หนึ่งลิตร	nùng lít
two litres of...	...สองลิตร	sö:ng lít
a bottle of...	...หนึ่งขวด	nùng kùat
a glass of...	...หนึ่งแก้ว	nùng gâew

Weights

100 grams of...	...หนึ่งขีด	nùng kìit
1/2 kilo of...	...ครึ่งกิโล	krûng gi-loo
one kilo of...	...หนึ่งกิโล	nùng gi-loo
two kilos of...	...สองกิโล	sö:ng gi-loo

Food

a slice of...	...หนึ่งชิ้น	...nùng chín
a dozen	...หนึ่งโหล	...nùng-löo
a box of...	...หนึ่งกล่อง	...nùng glò:ng
a carton of...	...หนึ่งคัทตอน	...nùng cut-tô:n

Miscellaneous

double	สองเท่า	sö:ng tâo
more	มาก	mâak
less	น้อย	nói
enough	เพียงพอ	piang-por
single	อันเดียว	an-diao

Numbers

In the Thai language, the noun doesn't change when it becomes a plural noun. For example, in English you would say 'two eggs', but in Thai you say 'two egg'. In Thai numbers, there are many classifiers used for objects and people. A classifier is a group to which

Reference

something belongs – a category. For instance, a cat might be classified as an animal, a carrot as a vegetable, or a house as a building. If you are not sure which classifier to use, you can use the word 'an/อัน' (thing) with most of the objects.

0	ศูนย์	süun
1	หนึ่ง	nùng
2	สอง	sö:ng
3	สาม	säam
4	สี่	sìi
5	ห้า	hâa
6	หก	hòk
7	เจ็ด	jèt
8	แปด	bpàet
9	เก้า	gâao
10	สิบ	sìp
11	สิบเอ็ด	sìp-èt
12	สิบสอง	sìp-sö:ng
13	สิบสาม	sìp-säam
14	สิบสี่	sìp-sìi
15	สิบห้า	sìp hâa

16	สิบหก	sìp hòk
17	สิบเจ็ด	sìp jèt
18	สิบแปด	sìp bpàet
19	สิบเก้า	sìp gâao
20	ยี่สิบ	yîi sìp
30	สามสิบ	säam-sìp
40	สี่สิบ	sìi sìp
50	ห้าสิบ	hâa-sìp
60	หกสิบ	hòk-sìp
70	เจ็ดสิบ	jèt-sìp
80	แปดสิบ	bpàet-sìp
90	เก้าสิบ	gâao-sìp
100	หนึ่งร้อย	nùng-ró:i
200	สองร้อย	sö:ng-ró:i
300	สามร้อย	säam-ró:i
400	สี่ร้อย	sìi-ró:i
500	ห้าร้อย	hâa-ró:i
1000	หนึ่งพัน	nùng-pan
2000	สองพัน	sö:ng-pan
3000	สามพัน	säam-pan
10,000	หนึ่งหมื่น	nùng-mùun

Reference

100,000	หนึ่งแสน	nùng-säen		
1,000,000	หนึ่งล้าน	nùng-láan		

1st	อันดับหนึ่ง an-dàp-nùng	6th	อันดับหก an-dàp-hòk
2nd	อันดับสอง an-dàp-sö:ng	7th	อันดับเจ็ด an-dàp-jèt
3rd	อันดับสาม an-dàp-säam	8th	อันดับแปด an-dàp-bpàet
4th	อันดับสี่ an-dàp-sìi	9th	อันดับเก้า an-dàp-gâao
5th	อันดับห้า an-dàp-hâa	10th	อันดับสิบ an-dàp-sìp

Days and months

Days วัน wan

Monday	วันจันทร์	wan-jan
Tuesday	วันอังคาร	wan-ang-kaan
Wednesday	วันพุธ	wan-pút
Thursday	วันพฤหัสบดี	wan-pá-rú-hàt- sa-bo:-dii

Friday	วันศุกร์	wan-sùk
Saturday	วันเสาร์	wan-säo
Sunday	วันอาทิตย์	wan-aa-tít
Weekend	วันหยุด เสาร์อาทิตย์	wan yùt säo- aa-tít

Months เดือน duan

January	มกราคม	má-gà-raa-kom
February	กุมภาพันธ์	gum-paa-pan
March	มีนาคม	mii-naa-kom
April	เมษายน	mee-säa-yon
May	พฤษภาคม	prút-sa-paa-kom
June	มิถุนายน	mí-tù-naa-yon
July	กรกฎาคม	gà-rá-gà-daa-kom
August	สิงหาคม	sing-häa-kom
September	กันยายน	gan-yaa-yon
October	ตุลาคม	dtù-laa-kom
November	พฤศจิกายน	prút-sà-jí-gaa-yon
December	ธันวาคม	tan-waa-kom

Reference

Seasons

หน้าร้อน   nâa rórn   **Hot season** (hot and humid; March to June)

หน้าฝน   nâa fön   **Rainy season** (heavy rainfall, not a good time to visit; July to October)

หน้าหนาว   nâa näao   **Cool season** (cool in the morning and at night, the best time to visit; November to February)

Time

The 24-hour clock is used in timetables, etc.

ตอนเช้า dtorn cháao	**a.m.** (morning)
ตอนเที่ยงวัน dtorn tîang wan	**It's midday**
ตอนบ่าย dtorn bàai	**p.m.** (afternoon)

English	Thai
It's...	**มันเป็นเวลา…**
	man bpen wee-laa...
It's 1 o'clock (afternoon)	**มันเป็นเวลาบ่ายหนึ่ง**
	man bpen wee-laa bàai nùng
It's 2 o'clock (afternoon)	**มันเป็นเวลาบ่ายสอง**
	man bpen wee-laa bàai sö:ng
What time is it?	**กี่โมงแล้ว**
	gìi moong láew?
9.00	**เก้าโมงตรง**
	gâao moong dtrong
9.10	**เก้าโมงสิบนาที**
	gâao moong sìp naa-tii
9.15	**เก้าโมงสิบห้านาที**
	gâao moong sìp hâa naa-tii
9.30	**เก้าโมงสามสิบนาที**
	gâao moong säam sìp naa-tii
9.45	**เก้าโมงสี่สิบห้านาที**
	gâao moong sìi sìp hâa naa-tii
9.50	**เก้าโมงห้าสิบนาที**
	gâao moong hâa sìp naa-tii
What is the date?	**วันนี้วันที่อะไร**
	wan níi wan-tîi a-rai?

Reference

It's 16 September 2006	**วันที่ 16 กันยายน 2006**
	wàn-tîi sìp hòk gan-yaa-yon sö:ng pan hòk
today	**วันนี้**
	wan níi
tomorrow	**พรุ่งนี้**
	prûng níi
yesterday	**เมื่อวานนี้**
	mûa waan níi

Time phrases

When does it begin/finish?	**เมื่อไหร่มันจะเริ่ม/เสร็จ**
	mûa-rài man jà rûrm/sèt?
When does it open/close?	**เมื่อไหร่มันจะเปิด/ปิด**
	mûa-rài man jà bpùrd/bpìd?
When does it leave?	**มันจะออกเมื่อไหร่**
	man jà òrk mûa-rài?
When does it return?	**มันจะกลับเมื่อไหร่**
	man jà glàb mûa-rài?
at 3 o'clock (afternoon)	**บ่ายสาม**
	bàai säam

before 3 o'clock (afternoon)	ก่อนบ่ายสาม gòːn bàai säam
after 3 o'clock (afternoon)	หลังบ่ายสาม läng bàai säam
in the morning	ตอนเช้า dtoːn cháao
this morning	เช้านี้ cháao níi
in the afternoon (until dusk)	บ่ายนี้ bàai níi
in the evening (after dusk)	ตอนเย็น dtoːn yen
in an hour's time	ภายในหนึ่งชั่วโมง paai-nai nùng chûa moong

Eating out

Eating places

A wide variety of food is available at all times of the day and night in Thailand, from fresh fruits to three course dinners. You can choose to eat in restaurants, the food courts in the shopping centres or at street shops. At street shops you sit down and eat right by the side of the road (be sure to drink bottled water and not the tap water from these shops).

ESTABLISHMENTS	TYPE OF FOOD SERVED
ร้านอาหารตามสั่ง ráan aa-häan-dtaam-sàng	fried rice and fried noodles
ร้านก๋วยเตี๋ยว ráan güai-dtïao	non-stir-fried noodles with soup or without soup

Thai	English
ร้านข้าวมันไก่ ráan kâao-man-gài	steamed rice cooked with chicken soup, and served with boiled chicken
ร้านข้าวหมูแดง ráan kâao müu-daeng	rice topped with barbecued pork
ร้านข้าวหน้าเป็ด ráan kâao nâa-bpèt	rice topped with barbecued duck
ร้านข้าวขาหมู ráan kâao käa- müu	rice with stewed pork
ร้านอาหารซีฟู้ด ráan aa-häan-sea-food	seafood
ร้านผัดไทย ráan pàt-tai	traditional Thai noodles
คาเฟ่ kà-fé	variety of foods and alcohol and feature live music
ร้านกาแฟ ràan gaa- fae	hot tea and coffee, iced tea and coffee, and other soft drinks

ภัตตาคาร pat-dtaa-kaan	variety of foods, they offer a higher standard of service than other establishments
ผับ/ไนท์คลับ pub/night-club	variety of foods and alcohol and feature live music
คาราโอเกะ kaa-raa-o-gè	variety of foods and alcohol and feature karaoke
ร้านไอศครีม ràan ai-sa-kriim	ice cream
ร้านข้าวต้ม ràan kâao dtôm	rice soup
ร้านโจ๊ก ràan jók	**porridge rice** (for breakfast)
ร้านยำ ràan yam	Thai salads

In a bar/café

Since Thailand is a hot country, hot drinks are not popular. However, you can find teas and coffees in hotel lobbies and some quality restaurants. Don't forget to try Thai iced coffee, Thai herbal drinks and Thai fruit juices such as guava nectar juice and coconut juice. The selling of alcohol is prohibited on Buddhist holy days, the King's birthday and the Queen's birthday.

What would you like?	คุณต้องการดื่มอะไร
	khun dtô:ng gaan dùum a-rai?
Hot coffee/hot tea please	กาแฟร้อน/ชาร้อน ครับ/ คะ
	gaa-fae ró:n/ chaa ró:n krab/kà
A ... please	...หนึ่งแก้ว
	...nùng gâew
2 ... please	...สองแก้ว
	...sö:ng gàew
3 ... please	...สามแก้ว
	...säam gàew
Do you have...?	คุณมี ... ไหม
	khun miiee ... mái?

Do you have beer?	คุณมีเบียร์ใหม
	khun mii beer mái?
Do you have brandy?	คุณมีบรันดีใหม
	khun mii brandy mái?
a bottle of sparkling water	ขอโซดาขวดหนึ่ง
	kör sò-daa kùat nùng
sparkling mineral water	โซดา
	sò-daa
still mineral water	น้ำแร่
	náam-râe
A cappuccino, please	ขอคาปูชิโน่ หนึ่งแก้ว ครับ/คะ
	kör ka-bpuu-chi-nôo nùng gâew krab/kà
A tea, please	ขอชาร้อนหนึ่งที่ครับ/ค่ะ
	kör chaa- ró:n nùng tîi krab/kà
with milk	ชาใส่นม
	chaa-sài-nom
with lemon	ชามะนาว
	chaa-ma-naow
with ice	ชาดำเย็น
	chaa-dam-yen
with sugar	ใส่น้ำตาลด้วย
	sài náam dtaan dûoy

133

without sugar	ไม่ใส่น้ำตาล
	mài sài náam dtaan
one more, please	ใส่น้ำตาลอีกหน่อยครับ/
	คะ
	sài náam dtaan ìik nòi krab/kà

Reading the menu

When eating in a restaurant, you may start with some appetizers such as deep-fried shrimps กุ้งทอด gûng tôrt, **spring rolls** ปอเปี๊ยะ bpo:-bpía, **deep-fried squid** ปลาหมึกชุบแป้งทอด bplaa-mùk chúp bpâeng tôrt, **chicken sàtée** ไก่สะเต๊ะ gài sà-dté, **Thai salad** ยำ yams, etc.

Usually soup is served with the main course. A cup of sweet dessert or some fruits follow the main course. Breads are not usually served with Thai food. Order your food in the order in which you want each dish to be served. Some restaurants may add a service charge of about 10–15% to your bill, so be sure to check before leaving tips.

menu	รายการอาหาร raai gaan aa-häan
appetizers	อาหารว่าง aa-häan wâang
Thai salad	ย่ำ yam
fried rice	ข้าวผัด kâao-pàd
stir-fry	ผัด pàd
soup	น้ำแกง náam-gaeng
curry	แกง gaeng
chili sauce	น้ำพริก náam- prík
dessert	ของหวาน kö:ng- wäan

In a restaurant

The menu, please	ขอเมนูด้วยครับ/ค่ะ
	kör menu dûoy krab/ká
Is there a set menu?	มีเมนูชุดไหม
	mii menu chút mái?
What is this?	นี่คืออะไร
	nîi kuu a-rai?

I'd like this	ฉันต้องการอันนี้
	chan dtô:ng gaan an níi
What is the speciality of the house?	อะไรที่อร่อยของร้านนี้
	a-rai tîi aròːy kŏːng ráan níi?
Excuse me!	ขอโทษนะครับ/คะ
	kŏr tôot ná krab/ká!
The bill, please	เก็บเงินด้วยครับ/ค่ะ
	gèb ngurn dûoy krab/ká
Some more rice/ water, please	ขอข้าว/น้ำ เพิ่มด้วยครับ/ คะ
	kŏr kâao/náam pûrm dûoy krab/ká
salt	เกลือ
	glua
pepper	พริกไทย
	prík-tai
Another bottle, please	ขออันนี้อีกขวด
	kŏr an níi ìik kùat
Another glass, please	ขออันนี้อีกแก้ว
	kŏr an níi ìik gâew

Vegetarian

Some restaurants sell vegetarian food all year round, but you will find more vegetarian food available during mid-October when the vegetarian festival **เทศกาลกินเจ** teet-sà-gaan gin-jee takes place.

I am vegetarian	**ฉันเป็นมังสวิรัต** chan bpen mang sà-vi-rát
I don't eat meat	**ฉันไม่กินเนื้อสัตว์** chan mâi gin núa-sàt
Is there meat in this?	**มีเนื้อสัตว์ในอาหารนี้หรือ เปล่า** mii núa-sàt nai aa-häan níi rüu bplàao?
What is there without meat?	**มีอาหารอะไรบ้างที่ไม่มี เนื้อสัตว์** mii aa-häan a-rai bâang tîi mâi mii núa-sàt?

Vegetarian dishes

ผัดไทยเจ pàd-tai-jee stir-fried Thai noodles with bean sprouts, tofu and crushed peanut

ผัดพริกมะเขือยาว pàd-prík-ma-küa-yaow stir-fried aubergine with red chilli, pepper and basil leaves

ต้มยำเห็ด dtôm-yam-hèt hot and sour mushroom soup

ข้าวผัดผักรวมมิตร kâao-pàd-pàk-ruam-mit fried rice with various vegetables

ข้าวผัดเผือก kâao-pàd-pùak fried rice with taro

แกงเขียวหวานเจ gaeng-kïao-wäan-jee green curry with various vegetables

แกงเผ็ดเจ gaeng-pèt-jee red curry with various vegetables

จับฉ่าย jàb-chàai steamed mixed vegetables

ผัดผักรวมมิตร pàd-pàk-ruam-mit stir-fried various vegetables

ผัดซีอิ๊วเจ pàd-sii-íao-jee stir-fried noodles with black soya-sauce

ก๋วยเตี๋ยวเจ güai-dtïao-jee stir-fried noodles with various vegetables and tofu

เต้าหู้ทอด dtâo-hûu-tôrt **deep-fried tofu served with sweet peanut sauce**

เผือกทอด pùak-tôrt **deep-fried taro served with sweet peanut sauce**

ปอเปี๊ยะทอด bpo:-bpía-tôrt **deep-fried spring roll served with plum sauce**

Wines and spirits

Some Thai beers are very popular with tourists, and Thai wines are also available at local restaurants, nightclubs, pubs, etc.

The wine list, please	ขอรายการไวน์ด้วยครับ/คะ kör raai-gaan wine dûoy krab/ká
Can you recommend a good wine?	คุณจะแนะนำไวน์ดีดีได้ไหม khun jà náe-nam wine dii dii dâai mái?
A bottle of...	...หนึ่งขวด ...nùng kùat

red/white wine	**ไวน์แดง/ไวน์ขาว**
	wine-daeng/wine-käao
A glass of...	**...หนึ่งแก้ว**
	...nùng gâew
a dry wine	**ไวน์แห้ง**
	wine-hâeng
a local wine	**ไวน์พื้นเมือง**
	wine-púun-muang
a sweet wine	**ไวน์หวาน**
	wine-wäan

Common dishes

Appetizers **อาหารว่าง** aa-häan wâang

ขนมจีบ kä-nöm-jìip steamed wonton (pork/shrimp)

ขนมปังหน้าหมู kä-nöm- bpang-nâa- müu deep-fried bread top with pork

เกี๊ยวกุ้ง gíao gûng deep-fried shrimp wonton

ทอดมันปลากราย tôrt-man- bplaa kraai fish cake

ทอดมันกุ้ง tôrt-man-gûng shrimp cake

หมูสะเต๊ะ müu-sà-dtê barbecued pork served
with peanut curry sauce

หมูย่าง müu-yâang barbecued pork

ปอเปี๊ยะ bpo:-bpía deep-fried spring roll (pork)

ปลาหมึกชุบแป้งทอด bplaa mùk chúp bpâeng tôrt
deep-fried squid

กุ้งชุบแป้งทอด gûng chúp bpâeng tôrt deep-fried
shrimps

เต้าหู้ทอด dtâo-hûu-tôrt deep-fried tofu

ปีกไก่ทอด bpìik gái-tôrt deep-fried chicken wings

Salad ยำ yam

ส้มตำ sôm dtam papaya salad (spicy and sour)

ยำถั่วพู yam tùa puu winged bean salad (sweet
and sour)

ยำสามกรอบ yam säam grorb **crispy squid,
shrimp and cashew nuts salad,** (spicy and sour)

ยำทะเล yam tà-lee seafood salad (spicy and sour)

ยำปูอัด yam bpuu àt crab salad (spicy and sour)

ยำไส้กรอก yam sâi gròrk pork sausage salad
(spicy and sour)

ย่าหมูยอ yam müu yor **Thai pork sausage salad (spicy and sour)**

ย่าวุ้นเส้น yam wún sên **glass noodle salad (spicy and sour)**

สลัด sà-làd **vegetable salad**

สลัดแขก sà-làd kèek **vegetable salad with peanut dressing**

สลัดทะเล sà-làd tà-lee **seafood salad (not spicy)**

Soup น้ำแกง náam-gaeng

ต้มยำ dtôm yam **delicious savoury soup with shrimps, mushrooms, lemongrass, and Thai chilli**

แกงจืดเต้าหู้ทรงเครื่อง gaeng jùut dtâo-hûu song krûang **tofu soup**

แกงจืดสาหร่ายทะเล gaeng jùut säa-ràai tà-lee **seaweed soup**

ต้มซุปไก่ dtôm soup gài **chicken soup with mixed vegetables**

Meat **เนื้อ** núa

เนื้อวัว núa-wua beef
เนื้อไก่ núa gài chicken
เนื้อหมู núa müu pork
เนื้อเป็ด núa bpèt duck

Fish and seafood **ปลาและอาหารทะเล**
bplaa láe aa-häan ta-lee

กุ้งมังกร gûng mang gorn lobster
ปลาหมึก bplaa mùk squid
กุ้ง gûng prawns
หอย hö:i mussels
ปลาดุก bplaa dùk catfish
ปลาช่อน bplaa chô:n serpenthead
ปู bpuu crab
ปลาน้ำจืด bplaa náam jùut freshwater fish
ปลาทะเล bplaa tà-lee saltwater fish

Desserts ของหวาน kŏ:ng wăan

กล้วยบวชชี glûai bùat-chii Thai bananas cooked
  with coconut milk

ฝอยทอง fŏ:i-torng egg yolk poured into hot syrup

เค้กนมสด cake nom sòt fresh milk cake

ลูกบัวถั่วแดงเย็น lûuk-bua tùa daeng yen sweet
  red bean and lotus tip in syrup

พายมะพร้าว paai mà-práao coconut pie

Eating out

Menu reader

ก

เกี๊ยวกุ้ง gíao gûng wonton shrimps

เกี๊ยวซ่า gíao sâa fried wonton (pork)

แกงเขียวหวาน gaeng kïao-wäan green curry (with chicken, beef or shrimps)

แกงเผ็ด gaeng pèt red curry

แกงเผ็ดเป็ดย่าง gaeng pèt bpèt yâang roast duck curry with cherry tomatoes

แกงเลี้ยง gaeng liang hot vegetable consommé with prawns

แกงจืดเต้าหู้ gaeng jùut dtâo-hûu tofu soup

แกงป่าลูกชิ้นปลากราย gaeng bpàa lûuk chín bplaa kraai jungle curry with fish balls

แกงมัสมั่น gaeng mat-sà-màn mat-sà-màn curry (yellow curry) with chicken/beef

แกงส้ม gaeng sôm hot and sour tamarind soup with fish

ไก่ผัดพริก gài pàt prík chicken with Thai chilli

ไก่ผัดพริกขิง gài pàt prík kïng chicken with string beans in dry red curry

ไก่ย่าง gài yâang barbecued chicken

ไก่ห่อใบเตย gài hòr bai dteei chicken nuggets wrapped in Toey leaves (pandon leaves)

ไก่อบน้ำแดง gài òp náam daeng steamed chicken in a clay pot

ไก่อบน้ำผึ้ง gài òp náam pûng steamed chicken with honey

กะหล่ำปลี gà-làm-bplii cabbage

กาแฟ gaa-fae coffee

กาแฟเย็น gaa-fae yen iced coffee

กาแฟสำเร็จรูป gaa-fae säm-rèt- rûub instant coffee

กุ้งเผา gûng päo barbecued shrimps

กุ้งแช่น้ำปลา gûng châe náam bplaa raw shrimps in fish sauce and Thai chilli

กุ้งชุบแป้งทอด gûng chúp bpâeng tôrt deep-fried shrimps

กุ้งมังกร gûng mang gorn lobster

กุ้งอบวุ้นเส้น gûng òp wún sên steamed shrimps and glass noodles in a clay pot

ข

ไข่ต้ม kài dtôm boiled eggs

เข้มข้น kêm-kôn strong taste

ข้าว kâao steamed rice

ข้าวเหนียว kâao-nïao steamed sticky rice

ข้าวเหนียวหมูย่าง kâao-nïao müu yâang
  steamed sticky rice with barbecued pork

ข้าวคลุกกะปิ kâao klúg gà-pi shrimp paste fried
  rice with condiments

ข้าวต้ม kâao dtôm rice soup

ข้าวผัดปู kâao pàt bpuu crab fried rice

ข้าวอบสับปะรด kâao òp sàp-bpa-rót pineapple
  fried rice

ค

คะน้าผัดน้ำมันหอย kà-náa pàt náam man hö:i
  stir-fried Chinese kale with oyster sauce

คะน้าผัดปลาเค็ม kà-náa pàt bplaa kem stir-fried
  Chinese kale with salty fish

ง

เงาะ ngó: rambutan

จ

จับฉ่าย jàb-chàai steamed mixed vegetables with pork or chicken

โจ๊ก jók porridge rice

ช

ชาดำเย็น chaa dam yen iced tea

ชามะนาว cha ma-naow lemon tea

ชาสมุนไพร chaa sa-mün-prai herb tea

ซ

ซาลาเปา sà-la-bpao Chinese bun

ซี่โครงหมูสามรส sîi-kroong müu säam rót sweet and sour pork ribs

ซี่โครงหมูย่าง sîi-kroong-müu-yâang barbecued pork ribs

ซีอิ๊วขาว sii-íu-käao soy bean sauce

ซุปเห็ด soup hèt mushroom soup

ซุปมะเขือเทศ soup má-küa-têet tomato soup

ซุปหน่อไม้ soup nòr màai young bamboo shoot salad (spicy)

แซนวิชทูน่า sand-wit-tuu-nâa tuna sandwich

ต

แตงโม dtaeng-moo watermelon

แตงกวา dtaeng-gwaa cucumber

ต้มข่าไก่ dtôm kàa gài lemongrass soup with
coconut milk and chicken

ต้มยำกุ้ง dtôm yam gûng spicy lemongrass soup
with river prawns

ตำส้มโอ dtam sôm-oo spicy pomelo salad

ท

ทอดมันกุ้ง tôrt man gûng shrimp cake

ทอดมันปลากราย tôrt man bplaa kraai fish cake

ทับทิม táb-tim pomegranate

ทุเรียน tú-rian durian

น

เนื้อแดดเดียว núa dàet diao deep-fried beef

เนื้อตุ๋น núa dtün steamed beef

น

น้อยหน่า nó:i nàa **custard apple**

น้ำแกง náam gaeng soup

น้ำแข็ง náam käeng ice

น้ำแข็งเปล่า náam käeng bplàao ice with water

น้ำแร่ náam râe mineral water

น้ำแอ๊ปเปิ้ล náam apple apple juice

น้ำดื่ม náam dùum drinking water

น้ำตาล náam dtaan **sugar**

น้ำตาลสด náam dtaan sòt **sugar palm sap**

น้ำปลา náam bplaa **fish sauce**

น้ำผลไม้ náam pönla-máai **fruit juice**

น้ำผึ้ง náam-pûng **honey**

น้ำฝรั่ง náam fa-ràng **guava juice**

น้ำพริกกะปิ náam prík gà pi **shrimp paste dip**
  served with deep-fried mackerel

น้ำพริกหนุ่ม náam prík nùm **northern spicy dips**
  served with assorted vegetables

น้ำมะเขือเทศ náam má-küa-têet **tomato juice**

น้ำมะนาว náam ma-naow **lime juice**

น้ำมะพร้าวอ่อน náam mà-práao òrn **coconut**
  juice

น้ำมะม่วง náam má-mûang **mango juice**

น้ำมันมะกอก náam man mà-gò:k **olive oil**

น้ำลำใย náam lam yai **longan juice**

น้ำลิ้นจี่ náam lín jìi **lychee juice**

น้ำส้มสายชู náam sôm säai chuu **vinegar**

น้ำสับปะรด náam sàp-bpa-rót **pineapple juice**

น้ำองุ่น náam a-ngùn **grape juice**

บ

เบียร์ beer beer

บรั่นดี brandy brandy

บะหมี่เกี๊ยว bà mìi gíao egg noodle soup with
  wontons

บะหมี่หมูแดง bà mìi müu daeng egg noodle soup
  with barbecued pork

ป

ปลา bplaa fish

ปลาเก๋าราดพริก bplaa käo râat prík grouper fish
  with chilli, garlic and pepper (sweet and sour sauce)

ปลากะพงทอดกรอบ bplaa gà pong tôrt krorb
  deep-fried sea bass

ปลากะพงนึ่งมะนาว bplaa gà pong nûng ma-
  naow steamed sea bass with lime

ปลากราย bplaa graai chitala fish

ปลาช่อน bplaa chô:n Thai catfish

ปาท่องโก๋ bpaa tô:ng-göo Chinese doughnuts

ปลาสำลีเผา bplaa säm-lii päo grilled black
  banded trevally fish

ปลาหมึก bplaa mùk squid

ปลาหมึกเผา bplaa mùk päo grilled squid

ปลาหมึกทอด bplaa mùk tôrt deep-fried squid

ปูเผา bpuu päo grilled crab

ปูจ๋า bpuu jä steamed crab

ปูผัดผงกระหรี่ bpuu pàt pöng gà-rii crab with egg
  and curry sauce/garlic and pepper

เป็ดตุ๋นน้ำใส bpèt dtün náam säi steamed duck

เป็ดย่าง bpèt yâang grilled duck

ผ

ผลไม้ pönla-máai fruit

ผักกาดแก้ว pàk gàad-gâew iceberg lettuce

ผัดเปรี้ยวหวาน pàt bprîao-wäan stir-fried
  vegetables with shrimps (sweet and sour)

ผัดเผ็ดปลาดุก pàt pèt bplaa dùk deep-fried
  catfish topped with chilli sauce

ผัดเม็ดมะม่วงหิมพานต์ pàt mét má-mûang
hïm mà paan chicken stir-fried with cashew nuts
and dried chilli

ผัดไทย pàt tai Thai noodles

ผัดซี่อิ๊ว pàt sii-íu fried rice noodles with soy sauce

ผัดถั่วงอกเต้าหู้หมูสับ pàt tùa ngò:k dtâo-hûu
  müu sàb stir-fried tofu with bean sprouts

ผัดถั่วลันเตา pàt tùa lan-dtao stir-fried snow
  peas with shrimp
ผัดผักรวมมิตร pàt pàk ruam mit stir-fried
  vegetables
ผัดวุ้นเส้น pàt wún sên stir-fried glass noodles
  with eggs

พ

แพนเค้ก paan-cake pancake
แพนง pà-naeng sweet curry with meat
พริกไทย prík tai black pepper
พริกขี้หนู prík kîi nüu Thai chilli (very spicy)
พริกน้ำปลา prík náam bplaa chilli in fish sauce
พริกป่น prík bpòn crushed chilli

ภ

ภัตตาคาร pát-dtaa-kaan restaurant

ย

แยม yaem jam
แยม ผลไม้ yaem pönla-máai fruit jam
ยำถั่วพู yam tùa puu spicy winged bean salad
ยำปลาดุกฟู yam bplaa dùk fuu deep-fried minced
  catfish with spicy mango salad

ยำปลาหมึก yam bplaa mùk **spicy squid salad**

ยำผักกะเฉด yam pàk ga-chèet **spicy water mimosa salad**

ยำวุ้นเส้น yam wún sên **spicy glass noodle salad with seafood**

ส

เสต็ก steak **steak**

สตรอเบอรี่ sa-dtror-bur-rii **strawberries**

ส้ม sôm **orange**

ส้มเขียวหวาน sôm kïao-wäan **sweet orange**

ส้มโอ sôm-oo **pomelo**

ส้มตำ sôm dtam **spicy papaya salad**

สลัด sà-làd **salad**

สลัดกุ้ง sà-làd gûng **shrimp salad**

สับปะรด sàp-bpa-rót **pineapple**

สุกี้ยากี้ suu-kîi-yaa-kîi **sukiyaki**

ล

ลาบไก่ lâab gài **hot chicken salad**

ลำไย lam-yai **longan**

ลิ้นจี่ lín jìi **lychee**

ว

วิสกี้ whisky whisky

ห

หน่อไม้ nòr màai young bamboo shoot

หน่อไม้ฝรั่งผัดใส่กุ้ง nòr màai fa-ràng pàt sài
  gûng stir-fried asparagus with shrimps

หมี่กรอบ mìi kròrb crispy sweet and sour rice
  noodles

หมูสะเต๊ะ müu sa-dté barbecued pork served with
  peanut curry sauce

หมูทอดกระเทียมพริกไทย müu tôrt grà-tiam
  prík tai pork with garlic and pepper

หอยแมงภู่อบหม้อดิน hö:i maeng-pûu òp môr
  din steamed mussels in a clay pot

หอยทอด hö:i tôrt crispy mussels

ห่อหมกทะเล hòr-mòk tà-lee steamed seafood
  curry paté

อ

องุ่น a-ngùn grapes

แอ๊ปเปิ้ล apple apple

ฮ

แฮม ham ham

Grammar

Sentence structure

• •

The basic Thai sentence structure is the same as in English: subject + verb + object. There is no gap to indicate separate syllables, words or sentences. Vowels are written above, below, before or after the consonant that they relate to.

Pronouns

• •

There is no difference in the form of pronouns in Thai when used as subject or object. However, there are many pronouns in the Thai language for the pronoun 'I/me'. The choice depends on the gender of the speaker.

I/me	ฉัน	chan
		chan is used by both males and females when speaking to friends.
	ผม	pöm
		pöm is used by males only. pöm is a polite word to use.
	ดิฉัน	di-chan
		di-chan is used by females only. Again, it is a polite word.
you	คุณ	khun
we/us	เรา	rao
he/him	เขา	käo
she/her	เธอ	tur
they/them	พวกเขา	puag-käo
it	มัน	man
		man is a pronoun normally used for referring to animals – and everything other than humans.
children	หนู	nüu

Verbs

•••

Verbs are not modified for different tenses, plurals or gender. There is no article such as 'a', 'an' or 'the'. The Thai language uses either the context or adverbs of time to indicate the period of time of an activity. The following are the common words used to indicate tenses.

Present continuous tense

กำลัง gamlang = verb 'to be' + verb(ing).
For example:

I am going to Pattayaa. ผมกำลังไปพัทยา
pöm gamlang bpai pattaya

Future tense

ja ja + verb + period of time (not required).
For example:

I will go to Pattaya next week
ผมจะไปพัทยาอาทิตย์หน้า pöm ja bpai
pattaya aa-tíd nâa

Past tense

It is very simple to form the past tense in Thai. You add the period of time to indicate the past. For example:

I went to Pattaya yesterday

ผมไปพัทยาเมื่อวานนี้ pöm bpai pattaya mûa waan níi

Adjectives

In the English language, adjectives are usually placed in front of the nouns they modify. In the Thai language, on the other hand, adjectives come after the nouns they describe. For example:

Chiang Mai is a beautiful city

เชียงใหม่เป็นเมืองสวย chiang mai bpen muangng süay

Negatives

• •

The word ไม่ mâi is used in a negative sentence.
We place the word ไม่ mâi in front of the verb in
the sentence. For example:

I am hungry ฉันหิวข้าว chan hïu kâao

I am not hungry ฉันไม่หิวข้าว chang mâi hïu
kâao

He likes spicy food เขาชอบอาหารเผ็ด
kâo chô:p aa-hään pèt

He does not like spicy food
เขาไม่ชอบอาหารเผ็ด kâo mâi chô:p aa-hään
pèt

She wants to go shopping เธออยากไปซื้อของ
turr yàak bpai súu kö:ng

She doesn't want to go shopping
เธอไม่อยากไปซื้อของ tur mâi yàak bpai súu
kö:ng

Questions

• •

Unlike in the English language, in Thai the question words are placed at the end of the sentence. The structure is subject + verb + object + question word. There is no need to put a question mark at the end of the sentence. The following are useful Thai question words:

what	อะไร	a-rai
when	เมื่อไหร่	mûa-rài
where	ที่ไหน	tîi nǎi
why	ทำไม	tam-mai
how	อย่างไร	yàang-rai
who/whom	ใคร	krai
whose	ของใคร	kǒ:ng krai

Prepositions

●●●●●●●●●●●●●●●●●●●●●●●●●●●●●●●●●●●●●

about	ประมาณ	bpra-maan
from	จาก	jàak
in, at	ใน, ที่	nai, tîi
on	บน	bon
under	ข้างใต้	kâang-dtâi
by/with:	โดย	duuoy
between	ระหว่าง	ra-wàang
without	ปราศจาก	bpràat-sa-jàak
except	ยกเว้น	yók-wén
inside	ข้างใน	kâang-nai
outside	ข้างนอก	kâang-nô:k

Public holidays

1 January	**New Year's Day**
13–15 April	**Songkran Festival** Thai New Year. Thai people all over the country celebrate at this time. On the streets people splash water at each other to cool themselves down during the hot season. The National Family Day also occurs at this time.
1 May	**National Labour Day** There is a celebration at Sanam Luang, Bangkok.
12 August	**HM the Queen's Birthday** The Queen's Birthday is also Mother's Day.
5 December	**HM the King's Birthday** Thai people gather at Sanam Luang in Bangkok on the evening of 5 December to celebrate this event.

English	Thai	
A		
a(an)	หนึ่ง	nùng
about	ประมาณ	bpra-maan
above	ข้างบน	kâang-bon
do you accept Visa®?	รับ	ráp
	คุณรับบัตรวีซ่าไหม	khun ráp bàt visa mái
accident	อุบัติเหตุ	ù-bàt-dti-hèet
ache	ปวด	bpùat
it aches	มันปวด	man bpùat
address	ที่อยู่	tîi yùu
admission charge	ค่าธรรมเนียม	kâa-tam-niam
adult	ผู้ใหญ่	pûu yài
aeroplane	เครื่องบิน	krûang bin
after	หลังจาก	paai-lǎng
afternoon	บ่าย	bàai
this afternoon	บ่ายนี้	bàai níi
in the afternoon	ช่วงบ่ายนี้	chûang bàai níi

English	Thai	
tomorrow	พรุ่งนี้	bàai prûng níi
afternoon		
again	อีกครั้ง	ìik kráng
age	อายุ	aa-yú
agent	ตัวแทน	dtua-taen
estate agent	ตัวแทนขาย	dtua-taen kǎai
	อสังหาริมทรัพย์	a-sǎng-hǎa-rim-ma-sáp
travel agent	บริษัททัวร์ท่องเที่ยว	bò-ri-sát tô:ng-tîao
ago	ผ่านไปแล้ว	pàan bpai láew
ahead	ข้างหน้า	kâang nâa
straight ahead	ตรงไปข้างหน้า	dtrong bpai kâang nâa
air conditioning	แอร์คอนดิชั่น	air-condition
airport	สนามบิน	sà-nǎam-bin
alarm	ระบบเตือนภัย	ra-bòb-dtuan-pai
alarm clock	นาฬิกาปลุก	naa-lí-gaa-bplùk
alcohol	เครื่องดื่มมึนเมา	krûang duum
	เหล้า	mun mao

Thai	English	Romanization
ไม่มีเหล้า	*without alcohol*	mâi miilâo
ผสม	all	pa-sŏm
ทั้งหมด	to be allergic to	táng-mòt
ภูมิแพ้	all right (OK)	puum-páe
ฉันไม่เป็นอะไร	I'm all right	chan mâi bpen a-rai
อยู่คนเดียว	alone	yùu kon diao
ตลอดไป	always	dta-lòrd bpai
รถพยาบาล	ambulance	rót-pa-yaa-baan
อเมริกา	America	a-mee-ri-gaa
คนอเมริกา	American	kon-a-mee-ri-gaa
และ	and	láe
โกรธ	angry	gròot
ฉันโกรธ	I'm angry	chan gròot
อย่างอื่น	another	yàang ùun
เบียร์อีกขวด	another beer	beer ìik kùat
คำตอบ	answer	kam-tòrb
ตอบ	to answer	tòrb

Thai	English	Romanization
เครื่องตอบ รับอัตโนมัติ	answering machine	krûang tòrb ráp àt-tà-noo-mát
มด	ants	mót
บางไหม	any	bâang mái
อพาร์ตเมนท์	apartment	a-páat-mént
แอ็ปเปิ้ล	apple	apple
น้ำแอ็ปเปิ้ล	apple juice	náam apple
เมษายน	April	mee-sǎa-yon
แขน	arm	kǎen
ฉันเจ็บแขน	my arm hurts	chan jèb kǎen
โดนจับ	to arrest	doon jàb
ขาเข้า	arrivals	kǎa-kào
มาถึง	to arrive	maa tǔng
ศิลปิน	artist	sǐn-lá-bpin
ที่เขี่ยบุหรี่	ashtray	tîi lìa bu-rìi
โรคหืด	asthma	rôok-hùut
ที่	at	tîi
จู่โจม/ถ้ำรับ	attack	jùu-joom/ kam-rûrp

English – Thai

English	Thai	Pronunciation
heart attack	โรคหัวใจ	rôok hŭa-jai
attention	กำเริบ	kam-rêrp
attractive	ความสนใจ	kwaam-sŏn-jai
August	สวย/มีเสน่ห์	sŭoy/mi-sa-nèe
Australia	สิงหาคม	sĭng-hăa-kom
	ประเทศออส	bprà-têet-ót-t-sa-
	เตรเลีย	dtree-lia
Australian	คนออส	kon ót-sa-dtree-
	เตรเลีย	lia
automatic car	รถเกียร์อัตโนมัติ	rót-gìa-auto
away	จากไป	jàak bpai
please go away!	กรุณาไปให้	ka-ru-naa bpai
	พ้น	hâi pón
B		
baby	ทารก	taa-rók
baby food	อาหารทารก	aa-hăan taa-rók
babysitter	คนดูแลเด็ก	kon-duu-lae-dèk
back (of body)	หลัง	lăng
backpack	เป้	bpê

English	Thai	Pronunciation
bad	ไม่ดี	mâi dii
bag	กระเป๋า	grà-bpǎo
baggage	กระเป๋า	grà-bpǎo dum
	เดินทาง	taang
baker's	คนทำขนมปัง	kon tam ka-nŏm
		bpang
ball	ลูกบอล	lûuk-bo:n
bandage	ผ้าพันแผล	pâa-pan-plăe
bank	ธนาคาร	ta-naa-kaan
bar	บาร์	bar
barber	ช่างตัดผม	châang-dtàt-pŏm
bargain	ต่อรอง	dtòr rong
no bargaining	ไม่มีการต่อ	mâi mii gaan dtòr
	รอง	rorng
basket	ตะกร้า	dtà-grâa
bath	การอาบน้ำ	gaan-àap-náam
where is the	ห้องน้ำอยู่ที่	hô:ng áap-náam
bathroom?	ไหน	hô:ng náam yùu
with bathroom	มีห้องน้ำ	tîi năi
		mii hô:ng náam

English	Thai	
battery (for car)	แบ็ตเตอรี่รถ	bàet-tur-rî-rót
(for torch, camera)	ถ่านไฟฉาย	tàan-fai-chăai
bazaar	ตลาดนัด	dtà-làat-nát
be	เป็น	bpen
beach	ชายหาด	chaai-hàat
beautiful	สวย	sŭay
bed	เตียง	dtiang
double bed	เตียงคู่	dtiang-kûu
twin beds	เตียงเดี่ยวคู่	dtiang-diao-kûu
bedclothes	ผ้าปูที่นอน	pâa-bpuu-tîi-norn
bedroom	ห้องนอน	hông-norn
double bedroom	ห้องเตียงคู่	hông-dtiang-kûu
single bedroom	ห้องเตียงเดี่ยว	hông-dtiang-diao
bee	ผึ้ง	pûng
beef	เนื้อวัว	núa-wua
beer	เบียร์	beer
a glass of beer	เบียร์หนึ่งแก้ว	beer nùng gâew
a bottle of beer	เบียร์หนึ่งขวด	beer nùng kùat
before	ก่อนหน้า	gòn nâa
before 4 o'clock	ก่อนสี่โมง	gòn sìi moong

English	Thai	
before dinner	ก่อนอาหารค่ำ	gòn aa-hăan kâm
to begin	เริ่ม	rûrm
behind	ข้างหลัง	kâang lăng
to believe	เชื่อ	chûa
I don't believe	ฉันไม่เชื่อคุณ	chăn mâi chûa khun
you	คุณ	khun
below	ข้างล่าง	kâang-lâang
belt	เข็มขัด	kém-kàt
money belt	กระเป๋าเข็มขัด	grà-bpăo kém-kàt
seat belt	เข็มขัดนิรภัย	kém-kàt ni-ra-pai
bend	ก้ม	gôm
beside	ข้าง	kâang
(next to)	ติดกับ	dtìd-kàp
best	ดีที่สุด	dii-tîi-sùt
better (than)	ดีกว่า	dii-gwàa
bicycle	จักรยาน	jàk-grà-yaan
big	ใหญ่	yài
bigger	ใหญ่กว่า	yài gwàa

English – Thai

English – Thai

English	Thai	
biggest	ใหญ่ที่สุด	yài tîi sùt
bill (invoice)	ใบเก็บเงิน	bai-gèb ngurm
bin (for rubbish)	ถังขยะ	tǎng kà-yà
bird	นก	nók
birthday	วันเกิด	wan-gùrt
happy birthday!	สุขสันต์วันเกิด	sùk-sǎn wan-gùrt
birthday card	การ์ดวันเกิด	gáat wan-gùrt
biscuits	บิสกิต	biscuit
a little bit	นิดหน่อย	níd-nòi
bite (insect, dog)	กัด	gàt
bitter (taste)	ขม	kǒm
black	ดำ	dam
blanket	ผ้าห่ม	pâa-hòm
to bleed	เลือดออก	lûat òrk
blind (person)	ตาบอด	dtaa-bòrt
blinds (on window)	ที่กันแสง	tîi-gan-sǎeng
blister	แผลพุพอง	plàe pú-porng

English	Thai	
blocked	ตัน	dtan
the sink is blocked	อ่างอันนี้ตัน	àang an níi dtan
blood	เลือด	lûat
blood group	เลือดกรุ๊ป	lûat-group
blood pressure	ความดันเลือด	kwaam dan lûat
blue	สีฟ้า	sǐi fáa
boarding card	บัตรผ่านประตู	bàt pàan bpra-tuu
boat	เรือ	ruua
boat trip	เดินทางทางเรือ	durn-taang taang ruua
boiled (food)	ต้ม	dtôm
bone	กระดูก	grà-dùuk
book	หนังสือ	nǎng-sǔu
to book	จอง	jorng
I've booked	ฉันจองไว้แล้ว	chan jorng wái láew
booking	การจอง	gaan jorng
bookshop	ร้านหนังสือ	ráan nǎng-sǔu
boots	ที่โชว์สินค้า	tîi show sín-káa

English	Thai	Pronunciation
boring	หน้าเบื่อ	nâa-bùa
it's boring	มันน่าเบื่อ	man nâabùa
both	อื้มสองอันนี้	kûu
I'd like both		chan chɔ̂p táng kûu
bottle	ขวด	kùat
a bottle of water	น้ำหนึ่งขวด	náam nùng kùat
a bottle of wine	ไวน์หนึ่งขวด	wine nùng kùat
bottle opener	ที่เปิดขวด	tîi bpə̀rd kùat
box	กล่อง	glòng
box office	ห้องขายตั๋ว	hɔ̂ng kǎai dtǔa
boy	เด็กผู้ชาย	dèk pûu chaai
boyfriend	แฟน	faen
brandy	บรั่นดี	brandy
bread	ขนมปัง	ka-nǒm bpang
to break	หัก	pàk
to break down (car)	รถเสีย	rót sia
breakfast	อาหารเช้า	aa-hǎan cháao

English	Thai	Pronunciation
breakfast included	รวมอาหารเช้า	ruam aa-hǎan cháao
to breathe	หายใจ	hǎai-jai
bring	นำ	nam
British	อังกฤษ	ang-grìt
I'm British	ฉันเป็นคนอังกฤษ	chan bpen kon ang-grìt
brochure	แผ่นโฆษณาถึง	pàen-koo-sà-naa
broken	เสีย	sia
broken down (car, machine)	เสีย	sia
brother (elder)	พี่ชาย/	pîi-chaai/
brother/younger brother)	น้องชาย	nɔ́ng-chaai
brown	สีน้ำตาล	sǐi-náam-dtaan
brush	แปรง	bpraeng
bucket	ถังน้ำ	tǎng náam
bulb (light)	หลอดไฟ	lɔ̀rdt-fai
burglary	ปล้น	bplôn
burn	ไหม้	mâi

to burn	เผา	pǎo
burnt	ไหม้	mâi
it's burnt	มันไหม้	man mâi
bus	รถบัส	rót-bus
business	ธุรกิจ	tú-rá-gìt
bus station	สถานีรถเมล์	sa-tǎa-nii
		rót-mee
bus stop	ป้ายรถเมล์	bpâai rót-mee
busy	ยุ่ง	yûng
I'm busy	ฉันกำลังยุ่ง	chan gam-lang
		yûng
butcher's	คนขายเนื้อ	kon kǎai núa
butter	เนย	neei
to buy	ซื้อ	súu
by	โดย	duoy
by bus	โดยรถบัส	duoy rót-bus
by train	โดยรถไฟ	duoy rót-fai

C

café	ร้านกาแฟ	ráan gaa-fae
cake	เค้ก	cake
cake shop	ร้านเค้ก	ráan-cake
to call (on phone)	โทรหา	too-hǎa
camcorder	กล้องถ่ายหนัง	glô:ng tâai nǎng
camera	กล้องถ่ายรูป	glô:ng tâai rûub
to camp	ออกค่าย	ò:k-kâai
camp site	บริเวณค่าย	bo:-ri-ween kâai
no camping	ไม่มีการตั้ง	mâi mii gaan tâng
	ค่ายบริเวณนี้	kâai bo:-ri-ween
		nii
can (tin)	กระป๋อง	grà-bpǒ:ng
cancel	ยกเลิก	yók-lûrk
candle	เทียนไข	tian-kai
can opener	ที่เปิดกระป๋อง	tîi bpùrd grà-
		bpǒ:ng
car	รถยนต์	rót-yon
by car	โดยรถยนต์	duoy rót-yon
car park	ที่จอดรถ	tîi jò:rd rót

English	Thai	pronunciation
car seat (for child)	ที่นั่งเด็ก	tîi nâng dèk
car wash	ที่ล้างรถ	tîi láang rót
card	การ์ด	gáat
cards (playing)	ไพ่	pâi
carpet (rug)	พรม	prom
carry	ถือ	tǔu
cash	เงินสด	ngum-sòt
I have no cash	ฉันไม่มีเงินสด	chan mâi mii ngum-sòt
to cash	เบิกเงิน	bùrg-ngum
cash desk	โต๊ะเก็บเงิน	dtó gèb ngum
castle	ปราสาท	bpra-sàat
cat	แมว	maew
caution	ระวัง	rá-wang
cave	ถ้ำ	tâm
CD	ซีดี	sii-dii
CD player	เครื่องเล่นซีดี	krûang lên sii-dii
cemetery	ป่าช้า	bpàa-cháa
central	ศูนย์กลาง	sǔun glaang

English	Thai	pronunciation
central station	สถานีหลักกลาง	sa-tǎa-nii sǔun glaang
town centre	ใจกลางเมือง	jai glaang muang
certificate	ใบรับรอง	bai-ráp-rorng
chain	สายโซ่	sôo (to chain – lâam-sôo)
chair	เก้าอี้	gâo-îi
champagne	แชมเปญ	chaem-bpeen
change (loose coins)	เศษสตางค์	sèet-sa-taang
to change (money)	แลกเปลี่ยน	lâek-bplian
changing room	ห้องเปลี่ยนเสื้อผ้า	hôrng bplian sûa-pâa
charge (fee)	ค่าธรรมเนียม	kâa-tam-niam
cheap	ถูก	tùuk
check	เช็ค	chék
to check in	เช็คอิน	chék-in
cheers!	ไชโย	chai-yo
cheese	เนยแข็ง	neei-kǎeng

English – Thai

English	Thai	Pronunciation
chemist's	เกลั้อูกร	pee-sàt-cha-gorn
night duty	เกลั้อูกราเวร	pee-sàt-cha-gorn ween rôrb-dùk
chemist	ร้อมตึก	check
cheque	เช็ค	sà-mùt check
cheque book	สมุดเช็ค	check dum-taang
traveller's cheques	เช็คเดินทาง	
cherry	เชอร์ตี้	chur-rîi
chest (of body)	อก	òk
chewing gum	หมากฝรั่ง	màak-fà-ràng
chickenpox	อีสุกอีใส	ii-sùk-ii-sǎi
child	เด็ก	dèk
chips	มันฝรั่งทอด	man fà-ràng tôrt
chocolate	ช็อคโกแลต	chók-goo-láet
hot chocolate	ช็อคโกแลตร้อน	chók-goo-láet rórn
chop (meat)	สับ	sàp
Christmas	คริสต์มาส	krít-sa-mâat
church	โบสถ์	boot
cigar	ซิการ์	sí-gâa

English	Thai	Pronunciation
cigarettes	บุหรี่	bù-rìi
a packet of cigarettes	บุหรี่หนึ่งซอง	bù-rìi nùng sorng
cinema	หนัง	nǎng
where is the cinema?	โรงหนังอยู่ที่ไหน	roong-nǎng yùu tîi nǎi?
city	เมือง	muang
city centre	ใจกลางเมือง	jai glaang muang
clean	ความสะอาด	kwaam sà-àat
it's not clean	มันไม่สะอาด	man mâi sà-àat
climbing	ทางคลาน	tam kwaam sà-àat
to go climbing	สะอาด	sà-àat
clock	ปีน	bpiin
close	ไปปีนเขา	bpai bpiin kǎo
is it close by?	หางใกล้กัน	naa-li-gaa
to close	โกล	glâi
when does it close?	อยู่ใกล้ๆไหม	yùu glâi mái?
	ปิด	bpìd?
	มันปิดเมื่อไหร่	man bpìd mûa-rài?

English – Thai

English	Thai	
closed	ปิด	bpìd
clothes	เสื้อผ้า	sûa-pâa
coast	ฝั่งทะเล	fàng-tá-lee
coat	เสื้อคลุม	sûa-klum
cocoa	โกโก้	goo-gôo
cockroach	แมลงสาบ	má-laeng-sàap
coconut	มะพร้าว	má-práao
coffee	กาแฟ	gaa-fae
black coffee	กาแฟดำ	gaa-fae-dam
iced coffee	กาแฟเย็น	gaa-fae-yen
instant coffee	กาแฟสำเร็จรูป	gaa-fae-săm-rèt-rûub
coin	เหรียญ	rĭan
Coke®	โค้ก	Coke
cold	หวัด	wàt
I have a cold	ฉันเป็นหวัด	chan bpen wàt
to be cold	หนาว	năao
I'm cold	ฉันหนาว	chan năao
colour	สี	sĭi
comb	หวี	wĭi

English	Thai	
to come (arrive)	มาถึง	maa tŭng
come in!	เชิญมา	kâo-maa!
comfortable	สบาย	sà-baai
company (business)	บริษัท	bò-ri-sàt
compass	เข็มทิศ	kĕm-tít
complaint	ต่อว่า	dtòr-wâa
computer	คอมพิวเตอร์	com-pu-ter
concert	คอนเสิร์ต	con-cert
conditioner (for hair)	ครีมนวดผม	cream-nûat-pŏm
condoms	ถุงยาง	tŭng-yaang
conference	การประชุม	gaan bpra-chum
to confirm	ยืนยัน	yuun-yan
congratulations!	ยินดีด้วยครับ/ค่ะ	yin dii dûoy kràb/kà!
connection (train, plane)	ต่อ	dtòr
consulate	สถานกงสุล	sà-tăan-gong-sŭn

English – Thai

English	Thai	
British consulate	สถานกงสุลอังกฤษ	sà-tăan-gong-sŭn ang-grìt
American consulate	สถานกงสุลอเมริกา	sà-tăan-gong-sŭn a-mee-rí-gaa
contact lens	คอนแทคเลนส์	ko:n-tàek-len
contraceptive pill	ยาคุมกำเนิด	yaa-kum-gam-nùrt
to cook	ทำอาหาร	tam aa-hăan
cooker	คนทำอาหาร	kon tam aa-hăan
copy	การเอกสาร	tàai èek-gà-săan
to copy (photocopy)	การเอกสาร	tàai èek-gà-săan
corkscrew	ที่เปิดขวด	tîi bpùrd wine
corner	หัวมุม	hŭa mum
cot	เปล	bplee
cost	ราคา	raa-kaa
how much does it cost?	ราคาเท่าไหร่	raa-kaa tâo rài?
cotton (material)	ผ้าฝ้าย	pâa-fâai
to cough	ไอ	ai

English	Thai	
counter (desk)	เคาน์เตอร์	count-ter
country (not town)	ชนบท	chon-na-bòt
couple (two people)	สามีภรรยา	săamii-panrayaa
crash (collision)	ชน	chon
crash helmet	หมวกกันน็อก	mùak gan nók
cream (dairy)	ครีม	cream
credit card	เครดิตการ์ด	kree-dìt-gáat
to cry (weep)	ร้องไห้	ró:ng-hâi
cucumber	แตงกวา	dtaeng-gwaa
cup	ถ้วย	tûai
cushion	เบาะ	bò:
customs	ศุลกากร	sŭn-lá-gaa-gorn
customs	ด่านศุลกากร	dàan sŭn-lá-gaa-gorn
control		
cut	ตัด	dtàt
to cut	ตัด	dtàt
to cycle (bicycle)	ขี่จักรยาน	kìi jàk-grà-yaan
a cycle	วงจร	wong-jorn

English – Thai

English	Thai	Transliteration
D		
daily	ประจำวัน	bprà-jam-wan
damage	เสียหาย	sǐa hǎai
dance	การเต้นรำ	gaan dtên-ram
to dance	เต้นรำ	dtên-ram
danger	อันตราย	an-dta-raai
dangerous	อันตราย	an-dta-raai
dark	มืด	mûut
date (calendar)	วันที่	wan-tîi
date of birth	วันเกิด	wan gùrt
daughter	ลูกสาว	lûuk sǎao
day	วัน	wan
deaf	หูหนวก	hǔu-nùuak
decaffeinated coffee	กาแฟไม่มีคาเฟอีน	gaa-fae mâi mii kaa-fee-in
December	ธันวาคม	tan-waa-kom
deck chair	เก้าอี้ผ้าใบ	gâo-îi-pâa-bai
deep	ลึก	lúk
delay	ล่าช้า	lâa-cháa
delicious	อร่อย	aròy
this is delicious!	อันนี้อร่อยมาก	an níi aròy mâak
dentist	หมอฟัน	mǒr fan
dentures	ฟันปลอม	fan-bplorm
deodorant	ยาดับกลิ่นตัว	yaa-dàp-glìn-dtua
department store	ห้างสรรพสินค้า	Hâang sàp-pa-sǐn-káa
departures	ขาออก	kǎa òrk
deposit	ฝาก	fàak
dessert	ของหวาน	kǒ:ng-wǎan
detergent	ผงซักฟอก	pǒng-sák-fôrk
diabetic	โรคเบาหวาน	rôok-bao-wǎan
dialling code	รหัสโทรศัพท์	rà-hàt too-rá-sàp
diamond	เพชร	pét
diarrhoea	โรคท้องเสีย	rôok tó:ng-sǐa
diary	ไดอารี่	dai-aa-rîi
dictionary	พจนานุกรม	pót-jà-naa-nú-grom
diesel	ดีเซล	dii-sell

English	Thai	
diet	การควบคุม อาหาร	gaan kûap-kum aa-hǎan
I'm on a diet	ฉันกำลังลด อาหารอยู่	chan gamlang lót aa-hǎan
different	แตกต่าง	dtàek-dtàang
difficult	ยาก	yâak
it's difficult	มันยาก	man yâak
dinghy	เรือเล็ก	ruua lék
dining room	ห้องทานอาหาร	hô:ng taan aa-hǎan
dinner (evening meal)	อาหารค่ำ	aa-hǎan kâm
direct	ตรง	dtrong
direct flight	บินตรง	bin dtrong
directory (telephone)	สมุดโทรศัพท์	sà-mùt too-rá-sàp
dirty	สกปรก	sòk-gà-bpròk
disabled (person)	คนพิการ	kon pí-gaan
disco	เธค	tèk
discount	ส่วนลด	sùan lót
disease	โรค	rôok
disinfectant	ยาฆ่าเชื้อโรค	yaa-kâa-chúua-rôok
distilled water	น้ำกลั่น	náam-glàn
to dive	ดำน้ำ	dam náam
divorced	หย่า	yàa
I'm divorced	ฉันเป็นหม้าย	chan bpen mǎai
dizzy	เวียนหัว	wiian hǔa
I feel dizzy	ฉันรู้สึกเวียนหัว	chan rúu-sùk wiian hǔa
doctor	หมอ	mǒr
documents	เอกสาร	èek-gà-sǎan
dog	หมา	mǎa
doll	ตุ๊กตา	dtúk-gà-dtaa
door	ประตู	bpra-tuu
double bed	เตียงคู่	dtiang kûu
double room	ห้องคู่	hông kûu
downstairs	ชั้นล่าง	Chán lâang
dozen	หนึ่งโหล	nùng-lǒo
drain	ระบายน้ำ	rá-baai-náam

drawer	ลิ้นชัก	lín-chák
dress	กระโปรงชุด	gra-bproong-chút
drink	ดื่ม	dùem
to drink	การดื่ม	gaan dùem
drinking water	น้ำดื่ม	náam dùem
to drive	ขับ	kàp
driver	คนขับ	kon kàp
driving licence	ใบขับขี่	bai-kàp-kìi
to drown	จมน้ำ	jom náam
drug	ยา	yaa
drunk	เมา	mao
I'm drunk	ฉันเมา	chan mao
dry	ทำให้แห้ง	tam-hâi-hâeng
dry-cleaner's	ร้านซักแห้ง	ráan sák hâeng
dust	ฝุ่น	fùn
duty-free	ร้านสินค้าปลอดภาษี	ráan sin-káa bplòrt paa-sii

E

ear	หู	hŭu
earache	หูเจ็บ	hŭu jèb
I have earache	หูฉันเจ็บ	hŭu chan jèb
early	เช้าเมื่อ	cháao cháao
earrings	ต่างหู	dtàang- hŭu
earthquake	แผ่นดินไหว	pàen-din-wăi
east	ตะวันออก	dtà-wan-òrk
easy	ง่าย	ngâai
to eat	กิน	gin
egg	ไข่	kài
elastic band	ยางยืด	yaang-yûud
electric	ไฟฟ้า	fai-fáa
electric razor	มีดโกนไฟฟ้า	mîit-goon fai-fáa
e-mail	อีเมล	e-mail
embassy	สถานทูต	sa-tăan-tûut
American embassy	สถานทูต	sa-tăan-tûut
British embassy	อเมริกัน	a-mee-ri-gaa
	สถานทูตอังกฤษ	sa-tăan-tûut ang-grìt

English – Thai

English	Thai	Pronunciation
emergency	ฉุกเฉิน	chùk-chǔm
empty	ว่างเปล่า	wâang bplàao
end	จบ	jòp
engaged (to be married)	หมั้น	mân
it's engaged (phone, toilet)	มันไม่ว่าง	man mâi wâang
engine	เครื่องยนต์	krûang-yon
England	อังกฤษ	ang-grìt
English	คนอังกฤษ	kon ang-grìt
I'm English	ฉันเป็นคนอังกฤษ	chan bpen kon ang-grìt
enough	เพียงพอ	piang-por
it's not enough	มันไม่พอ	man mâi por
enquiry desk	ติดต่อสอบถาม	dtid-dtòr sòrb-tǎam
to enter	การเข้าไป	gaan kâo bpai
entertainment	การบันเทิง	gaan ban-tung
entrance	ทางเข้า	taang kâo
entrance fee	ค่าเข้า	kâa kâo

English	Thai	Pronunciation
envelope	ซองจดหมาย	so:ng-jòt-mǎai
escape	หลบหนี	lòp nǐi
fire escape	ทางหนีไฟ	taang-nǐi-fai
Europe	ยุโรป	yú-rôop
evening	ตอนเย็น	dtorn yen
this evening	เย็นนี้	yen níi
tomorrow evening	เย็นพรุ่งนี้	yen prûng níi
evening meal	อาหารเย็น	aa-hǎan yen
every	ทุกๆ	túk túk
every day	ทุกๆวัน	túk túk wan
every year	ทุกๆปี	túk túk bpii
everyone	ทุกๆคน	túk túk kon
excellent	ยอดเยี่ยม	yôt-yîam
exchange	แลกเปลี่ยน	lâek bplian
exchange rate	อัตราแลกเปลี่ยน	àt-dtraa lâek bplian
exciting	น่าตื่นเต้น	nâa-dtèun-dtên
excuse me!	ขอโทษครับ/คะ	kǒr-tôot krab/kà!

English	Thai		English	Thai	
exhibition	นิทรรศการ	ní-tát-sà-gaan	famous	มีชื่อเสียง	mii chûu-sĭang
exit	ทางออก	taang òrk	fan	แฟน	faen
where is the exit?	ทางออกอยู่ ที่ไหน	taang òrk yùu nǎi?	far	ไกล	glai
emergency exit	ทางออกฉุกเฉิน	taang òrk chùk-chĕrn	is it far?	ไกลไหม	glai mái?
			fare (train, bus, etc.)	ค่าโดยสาร	kâa duoy-sǎan
expensive	แพง	paeng	farm	ฟาร์ม	farm
to expire	หมดอายุ	mòt aa-yú	farmer	ชาวนา	chao-naa
to explain	อธิบาย	à-tí-baai	fashion	แฟชั่น	fae-chân
please explain	กรุณาอธิบาย	ga-rú-naa à-tí-baai	fast	เร็ว	reo
			fat (person)	อ้วน	ûan
extra	เพิ่ม	pôrm	father	พ่อ	pôr
eye	ตา	dtaa	my father	พ่อของฉัน	pôr kǒng chan
			father-in-law	พ่อตา	pôr dtaa
F			fault (defect)	มีตำหนิ	mii dtam-nì
face	หน้า	nâa	favourite	โปรดปราน	bpròot-bpraan
factory	โรงงาน	roong-ngaan	February	กุมภาพันธ์	gum-paa-pan
to faint	เป็นลม	bpen lom	feel	รู้สึก	rúu-sùk
to fall	ตก	dtòk	I feel sick	ฉันรู้สึกคลื่น ไส้	chan rúu-sùk klûun-sâi
family	ครอบครัว	krôrp-krua			

English – Thai

English – Thai

English	Thai	Pronunciation
I feel tired	จิตเหนื่อย	chan nùai
ferry	เรือข้ามฟาก	rua-kâam-fâak
few	เล็กน้อย	níd-nói
fiancé(e)	คู่หมั้น	kûu-mân
fill it up!	เติมให้เต็ม	dturm hâi dtem!
film	ฟิล์ม	film
filter	ที่กรอง	tîi grorng
to find	ค้นหา	kón-hǎa
fine (to be paid)	ค่าปรับ	kâa bpràp
fine (weather)	อากาศดี	aa-gàat dii
finish	เสร็จ	sèt
fire	ไฟ	fai
fire alarm	สัญญาณเตือนไฟ	sǎn-yaan dtuan fai
fire brigade	สถานีดับเพลิง	sà-tǎa-nii-dàp-plurng
fire exit	ทางหนีไฟ	taang nǐi fai
fireworks	พลุไฟ	plú-fai
first	ครั้งแรก	kráng râek

English	Thai	Pronunciation
the first train	รถไฟเที่ยวแรก	rót fai tîao râek
the first bus	รถบัสเที่ยวแรก	rót bus tîao râek
first aid	ปฐมพยาบาล	bpà-tǒm pa-yaa-baan
first class	ชั้นหนึ่ง	chán nùng
first floor	ชั้นหนึ่ง	chán nùng
fish	ปลา	bplaa
to fish	ตกปลา	dtòk bplaa
fisherman	คนจับปลา	kon jàb bplaa
fit	พอดี	por-dii
fix	ซ่อม	sô:m
flash (for camera)	แฟลช	flash
flat (apartment)	แฟลต	flat
flat	แบน	baen
flavour	รส	rót
flight	เที่ยวบิน	tîao-bin
flood	น้ำท่วม	náam-tûam
floor	ชั้น	chán

English	Thai	
flour	แป้ง	bpâeng
flower	ดอกไม้	dòk-máai
flu	ไข้หวัดใหญ่	kâi-wàt-yài
fly	บิน	bin
to fly	การบิน	gaan bin
fog	หมอก	mòrk
folder	แฟ้ม	fáem
to follow	ตาม	dtaam
food	อาหาร	aa-hǎan
foot	เท้า	táo
football (game)	ฟุตบอล	fút-bo:n
for	สำหรับ	sǎm-ràp
for me	สำหรับฉัน	sǎm-ràp chan
for sale	ขาย	kǎai
forbidden	ต้องห้าม	dtông hâam
forecast (weather)	พยากรณ์อากาศ	pa-yaa-gorn aa-gàat
foreign	คนต่างชาติ	kon dtàang-châat
forest	ป่า	bpàa
forever	ตลอดไป	dta-lòrd-bpai

English	Thai	
to forget	ลืม	luum
fork (for eating)	ส้อม	sôːm
forward(s)	ส่งต่อ	sòng dtòr
free (unoccupied)	ว่าง	wâang
(costing nothing)	ฟรี	frii
freezer	ช่องแช่เย็น	chôːng-châe-yen
French	คนฝรั่งเศส	kon fa-ràng-sèet
frequent	ถี่, บ่อย	tìi, bòːi
fresh	สด	sòt
is it fresh?	มันสดไหม	man sòt mái?
fresh fruit	ผลไม้สด	pôn-la-máai sòt
fresh vegetables	ผักสด	pàk sòt
fresh milk	นมสด	nom sòt
fresh fish	ปลาสด	bplaa-sòt
Friday	วันศุกร์	wan-sùk
fridge	ตู้เย็น	tûu-yen
fried (food)	ทอด	tôrt
friend	เพื่อน	pûan
from	จาก	jàak
		see GRAMMAR

English – Thai

front	ข้างหน้า	kâang nâa
front door	ประตูหน้า	bpra-dtuu nâa
frozen	แช่แข็ง	châe-kăeng
fruit	ผลไม้	pŏnla-mâai
fruit juice	น้ำผลไม้	náam pŏnla-mâai
fruit salad	สลัดผลไม้	sà-làd pŏnla-mâai
fuel	เชื้อเพลิง	chúa plung
full	เต็ม	dtem
furniture	เฟอร์นิเจอร์	fur-ni-ture

G

gallery (art)	ห้องแสดง	hôːng sa-daeng
	ศิลปะ	sĭn-lá-bpà
game (sport)	กีฬา	gii-laa
garden	สวน	sŭan
garlic	กระเทียม	grà-tiam
gas	แก๊ส	gas
gate	เวลา	taang-kâo
genuine	แท้	táe
German	คนเยอรมัน	kon yur-rà-man

Germany	เยอรมัน	yur-rà-man
to get	ได้	dâai
to get into	การเอารถเข้า	gaan kâo bpai sùu
to get on board	ขึ้นเรือ	kûn ruua
to get off	ลงรถ	long rót
(bus, etc.)		
gift	ของขวัญ	kɔ̌ːng-kwăn
girl	เด็กผู้หญิง	dèk pûu-yĭng
girlfriend	แฟน	faen
to give	ให้	hâi
(give back)	ให้กลับ	hâi glàb
give way	ให้ทาง	hâi taang
glass (for drink)	แก้ว	gâew
a glass of water	น้ำหนึ่งแก้ว	náam nùng gâew
a glass of wine	ไวน์หนึ่งแก้ว	wine nùng gâew
to go	ไป	bpai
to go back	กลับไป	glàb bpai
to go in	เข้าไป	kâo bpai
to go out	ออกไป	ɔ̀rk bpai
gold	ทอง	torng

English	Thai	Pronunciation
golf	กอล์ฟ	golf
golf ball	ลูกกอล์ฟ	lûuk golf
golf club	กอล์ฟคลับ	golf club
good	ดี	dii
goodbye	ไปก่อนนะ	bpai kòn ná
good day	สวัสดี	sà-wàd-dii
goodnight	ราตรีสวัสดิ์	raa-trii-sà-wàd
grandfather (paternal, maternal)	ปู่, ตา	bpùu, dtaa
grandmother (paternal, maternal)	ย่า, ยาย	yâa, yaai
grapes	องุ่น	a-ngùn
greasy	มัน	man
green	เขียว	kǐao
greengrocer's	ร้านขายผัก	ráan kǎai pàk
grey	สีเทา	sǐi tao
grilled	ย่าง	yâang

182 | 183

English – Thai

English – Thai

English	Thai	Transliteration
hand	มือ	muu
hand luggage	กระเป๋าถือ	grà-bpǎo tǔu
handbag	กระเป๋าถือขึ้นเครื่อง	grà-bpǎo muu tǔu
hand-made	ทำด้วยมือ	tam dûoy muu
to happen	เกิดขึ้น	gèrt kûn
what happened?	เกิดอะไรขึ้น	gèrt a-rai kûn?
happy	ความสุข	kwaam-sùk
hard (tough)	ยาก	yâak
hat	หมวก	mùak
he	เขา	kǎo
head	หัว	hǔa
headache	ปวดหัว	bpùat hǔa
I've got a headache	ฉันปวดหัว	chan bpùat hǔa
to hear	ได้ยิน	dâai yin
heart	หัวใจ	hǔa-jai
heating	ทำความร้อน	tam kwaam rórn
heavy	หนัก	nàk
height	ความสูง	kwaam-sǔung
hello	สวัสดี	Sa-Wad-Dii

English	Thai	Transliteration
help!	ช่วยด้วย	chûai dûoy!
to help	ช่วย	chûai
herbs	สมุนไพร	sà-mǔn-un-prai
here	ที่นี่	tîi-nîi
high	สูง	sǔung
high blood pressure	ความดันโลหิตสูง	kwaam-dan sǔung
high chair	เก้าอี้สำหรับเด็ก	dtó sǎm-ràp dèk
to hire	เช่า	châo
to hitch-hike	โบกรถ	bòok-rót
holiday	วันหยุด	wan yùd
home	บ้าน	bâan
honey	น้ำผึ้ง	náam-pûng
honeymoon	น้ำผึ้งพระจันทร์	náam pûng prá-jan
horse	ม้า	máa
hospital	โรงพยาบาล	roong-pa-yaa-baan
hot	ร้อน	rórn

English	Thai	Pronunciation
it's too hot	มันร้อนเกินไป	man rórn gurn bpai
hotel	โรงแรม	roong-raem
hour	ชั่วโมง	chûa-moong
house	บ้าน	bâan
how?	ยังไง?	yàang-rai?
how much?	เท่าไหร่?	tâo-rài?
how many?	จำนวนเท่าไหร่?	jam-nuan tâo-rài?
how are you?	คุณสบายดีหรือ?	khun sà-baai dii rǔu?
hungry	หิว	hǐu
I'm hungry	ฉันหิว	chan hǐu
hurry	เร็วเร็ว	reo reo
I'm in a hurry	ฉันกำลังรีบ	chan gamlang rîib
hurt	เจ็บ	jèb
it hurts	มันเจ็บ	man jèb
husband	สามี	sǎamii
my husband	สามีของฉัน	sǎamii kǒ:ng chan

English	Thai	Pronunciation
I	ฉัน	chan
ice	น้ำแข็ง	náam kǎeng
ice cream	ไอศกรีม	ai-sà-kriim
ice coffee	กาแฟเย็น	gaa-fae-yen
iced tea	ชาเย็น	cha-yen
iced water	น้ำเย็นป่นเปล่า	náam kǎeng bplàao
identification card	บัตรประจำตัว	bàt bpra jam dtua
ill	ป่วย	bpùai
I'm ill	ฉันป่วย	chan bpùai
immediately	โดยทันที	duoy tan-tii
important	สำคัญ	sǎm-kan
impossible	เป็นไปไม่ได้	bpen bpai mâi dâai
it's impossible	มันเป็นไปไม่ได้	man bpen bpai mâi dâai
included	รวม	ruam
indigestion	อาหารไม่ย่อย	aa-hǎan-mâi-yô:i
infection	อักเสบ	àk-seep

English – Thai

English	Thai	Pronunciation
information	ข้อมูล	kôr-moon
information office	ติดต่อสอบถาม	dtìd-dtòr
	ถาม	sòrb-tăam
injured	บาดเจ็บ	bàat-jèb
I've been injured	ฉันบาดเจ็บ	chan bàatjèb
insect	แมลง	ma-laeng
insect bite	แมลงกัด	ma-laeng gàt
insect repellent	ยากันแมลง	yaa-gan-ma-laeng
instant coffee	กาแฟสำเร็จรูป	gaa-fae săm-rèt-rûub
insurance	ประกัน	bpra-gan
interesting	น่าสนใจ	nâa-sŏn-jai
international	สากล	săa-gon
interpreter	เชิญ	lâam
to invite	เชิญ	churn
invoice	ใบส่งของ	bai-sòng-kŏng
Ireland	ประเทศไอร์แลนด์	bprà-têet-ai-laen
Irish	คนไอริช	kon-ai-rìsh

English	Thai	Pronunciation
iron (metal)	ธาตุเหล็ก	tâat lèk
iron (for clothes)	เตารีด	dtao-rîit
island	เกาะ	gò:
it	มัน	man
itch	คัน	kan
J		
jacket	เสื้อแจ็คเก็ต	sûa jàek-gét
leather jacket	เสื้อหนัง	sûa năng
jam (food)	แยม	yaem
January	มกราคม	má-ga-raa-kom
jar	กระปุก	grà-bpùk
jeans	ยีนส์	yiin
jellyfish	แมงกะพรุน	maeng-gà-prun
jewellery	เครื่องประดับ	krûang-bprà-dàb
Jewish	ยิว	yui
I'm Jewish	ฉันเป็นคนยิว	chan bpen kon yui
job	งาน	ngaan
joke	ล้อเล่น	lór-lên

English	Thai	
journalist	นักหนังสือ	nák-nǎng-sǔu-pim
	พิมพ์	
journey	การเดินทาง	gaan dɤɤn-taang
juice	น้ำผลไม้	náam pǒnla-máai
orange juice	น้ำส้ม	náam sôm
tomato juice	น้ำมะเขือเทศ	náam má-kǔa-têet
July	กรกฎาคม	gà-rá-gà-daa-kom
June	มิถุนายน	mí-tù-naa-yon
K		
to keep	เก็บ	gèb
key	กุญแจ	gun-jae
kind	ใจดี	jai dii
you're very kind	คุณใจดีมาก	khun jai dii mâak
to kiss	จูบ	jùup
kitchen	ห้องครัว	hông krua
knee	เข่า	kào
knife	มีด	mîit
to know	รู้	rúu

English	Thai	
I know	ฉันรู้	chan rúu
I don't know	ฉันไม่รู้	chan mâi rúu
L		
ladies' (toilet)	ห้องน้ำ	hông-nǎam
	สุภาพสตรี	sù-pàap-sà-dtrii
larger	ใหญ่กว่า	yài gwàa
lake	ทะเลสาบ	tà-lee sàap
lamp	โคมไฟ	koom-fai
land	จอด	jòt
landing	ลงจอด	long jòt
late	สาย	sǎai
sorry I'm late	ขอโทษที่มาสาย	Kǒr-tôot tîi sǎai
later	วันหลัง	wan lǎng
laundry	บริการซักรีด	bo-ri-gaan
service		sák-rît
lawyer	ทนาย	tá-naai
leather	หนัง	nǎng
to leave	จาก	jàak
left	ทิ้ง	tîng

English – Thai

English	Thai
left-luggage office	ที่ฝากสัมภาระ tîi dtìd-dtòr
leg	การขาหาม sǎm-paa-rá hǎai
lemonade	ขา kǎa
to lend	น้ำมะนาว náam ma-naow
to let (allow)	ให้ยืม hâi yuum
licence (driving)	ให้ hâi
lifeboat	ใบอนุญาต bai-à-nú-yâat
life jacket	เรือกู้ภัย ruua gûu-pai
lifeguard	เสื้อชูชีพ sûa-chuu-chîip
lift (elevator)	หน่วยกู้ภัย nùai gûu-pai
light (illumination)	ลิฟท์ lift
light bulb	ไฟส่องสว่าง fai sòrng sa-wàng
lighter (cigarette)	หลอดไฟ lòrd-fai
to like	ไฟแช็ก fai-shæ̂ek
I like coffee	ชอบ chôrp
	ฉันชอบกาแฟ chan chôrp gaa-fæe
I don't like	ฉันไม่ชอบ chan mâi chôrp
coffee	กาแฟ gaa-fæe
linen	ผ้าลินิน pâa linin

English	Thai
lipstick	ลิปสติ๊ก lip-sa-tíck
to listen to	ฟัง fang
litter (rubbish)	ขยะ kà-yà
little (small)	เล็ก lék
just a little,	ขอนิดเดียว kŏr níd-diao
please	ครับ/ คะ krảp/kà
to live	อาศัย aa-sǎi
I live in London	ฉันอาศัยที่ chan aa-sǎi tîi
	ลอนดอน London
lock	ล็อก lock
to lock	ทำการล็อก tam gaan lock
locker (for	ล็อกเกอร์ lock-ger
luggage)	
long	นาน naan
to look after	ดูแล duu-lae
someone	
to look for	มองหา mo:ng-hǎa
lost	หาย hǎai
lot	มาก mâak
a lot	มากมาก mâak mâak

English	Thai	Transliteration
lotion	โลชั่น	lo-tion
loud	ดัง	dang
to love	รัก	rák
I love you	ฉันรักคุณ	chan rák khun
lovely	น่ารัก	nâa-rák
lucky	โชคดี	chôok-dii
luggage	กระเป๋าเดินทาง	grà-bpáo durn taang
lunch	อาหารกลางวัน	aa-hăan glaang wan
M		
maid	คนรับใช้	kon ráp chái
main course (of meal)	อาหารหลัก	aa-hăan-làk
to make	ทำ	tam
man	ผู้ชาย	pûu chaai
manager	ผู้จัดการ	pûu-jàt-gaan
map	แผนที่	păen-tîi
March	มีนาคม	mii-naa-kom

English	Thai	Transliteration
married	แต่งงาน	dtàeng-ngaan
match (game)	เกมส์	game
matches (light)	ไม้ขีด	máai-kìit
maximum speed	ความเร็วสูงสุด	kwaam reo súung sùt
May	พฤษภาคม	prút-sa-paa-kom
meal	อาหาร	aa-hăan
mean	หมายถึง	măai tŭng
measure	วัด	wát
meat	เนื้อ	núa
medicine	ยา	yaa
to meet	พบ	pób
meeting	การประชุม	gaan bpra-chum
menu	รายการ	raai-gaan
message	ข้อความ	kŏr-kwaam
meter (taxi)	มิเตอร์	mi-dtur
microwave (oven)	ไมโครเวฟ	mai-cro-wave
midday	เที่ยงวัน	tîang wan
middle	กลาง	glaang

English – Thai

English – Thai

English	Thai	
midnight	เที่ยงคืน	tîang kuun
milk	นม	nom
mineral water	น้ำแร่	náam râe
mints	ใบสะระแหน่	bai-sa-rà-nàe
minute	นาที	naa-tii
mirror	กระจก	grà-jòk
miss (plane, train)	พลาด	plâad
missing (thing)	หาย	hǎai
mistake	ผิด	pìd
Monday	วันจันทร์	wan-jan
money	เงิน	ngurn
month	เดือน	duan
moon	พระจันทร์	prá-jan
more	มากขึ้น	mâak kûn
some more...	ขอเพิ่มอีกหน่อย	kŏr pûrm ìik nòi
morning	ตอนเช้า	dtorn cháao
in the morning	ในตอนเช้า	nai dtorn cháao
this morning	เช้านี้	cháao níi

English	Thai	
tomorrow	พรุ่งนี้	prûng níi
morning	เช้า	cháao
mosque	สุเหร่า	sù-rào
mosquito net	มุ้ง	múng
mosquitoes	ยุง	yung
mother	แม่	mâe
mother-in-law	แม่ยาย	mâe-yaai
motorway	ทางด่วน	taang dùan
mountain	ภูเขา	puu-kǎo
mouse	หนู	nǔu
moustache	หนวด	nùat
mouth	ปาก	bpàak
much	มาก	mâak
how much?	เท่าไหร่	tâo-rài?
too much	มากไป	mâak bpai
(too expensive)	แพงเกินไป	man paeng gurn bpai
museum	พิพิธภัณฑ์	pí-pít-ta-pan
music shop	ร้านเพลง	ráan pleeng
Muslim	อิสลาม	it-sa-laam

| mustard | มัสตาร์ด | mát-sa-tàad |

N

nail (metal)	ตะปู	dtà-bpuu
nail polish	น้ำยาทาเล็บ	náam-yaa-taa-lép
nail polish remover	น้ำยาล้างเล็บ	náam-yaa-láang lép
name	ชื่อ	chûu
my name is	ฉันชื่อ	chan chûu
napkin	ผ้าเช็ดปาก	pâa chét bpàak
narrow	แคบ	kâep
nationality	สัญชาติ	sǎn-châat
navy blue	สีกรมท่า	sǐi krom-mà-tâa
near	ใกล้	glâi
is it near?	มันใกล้ไหม?	man glâi mái?
necessary	จำเป็น	jam-bpen
neck	คอ	kor
to need	ต้องการ	dtô:ng gaan
I need...	ฉันต้องการ	chan dtô:ng gaan...

I need a car	ฉันต้องการรถ	chan dtô:ng gaan rót
I need to go	ฉันต้องจะไป	chan dtô:ng bpai
needle	เข็ม	kěm
neighbour	เพื่อนบ้าน	pûan bâan
nephew	หลานชาย	lǎan-chaai
never	ไม่เคย	mâi keei
new	ใหม่	mài
news	ข่าว	kàao
newspaper	หนังสือพิมพ์	nǎng-sǔu-pim
New Year	ปีใหม่	bpii mài
New Zealand	นิวซีแลนด์	niu-sii-laen
next	ต่อไป	dtòr bpai
next to	ติดกับ	dtìd-gàb
nice	ดี	dii
it's very nice	มันดีมาก	man dii mâak
niece	หลานสาว	lǎan sǎao
night	กลางคืน	glaang-kuun
last night	เมื่อคืน	mûa kuun
nightclub	ไนท์คลับ	night-club

English – Thai

no	ฉันไม่	mâi
no, thanks	ไม่ครับ/ค่ะ	mâi krab/kà
	ขอบคุณ	kòrb-kun
noisy	หนวกหู	nùak hùu
non-alcoholic	ไม่มีแอลกอฮอล์	mâi mii kò:ng
a non-alcoholic	สัมนา	mun-mao
drink	เครื่องดื่มที่ไม่	krûang dùum mâi
	ผสมแอลกอฮอล์	mii kò:ng
none	ไม่มี	mun-mao
there's none	เหลือ	mâi mii
left	ไม่มีอะไร	mâi mii a-rai-lùa
non-smoking	ห้ามสูบบุหรี่	hâam sùub-bu-rìi
	เหลือ	nùa
north	เกาะเหนือ	gò: ai-laen nùa
Northern	แถบตอนเหนือ	
Ireland		
nose	จมูก	jà-mùuk
not	ไม่	mâi
notebook	โน้ตบุ๊ค	note-book
nothing	ไม่มีอะไร	mâi mii a-rai

November	พฤศจิกายน	prút-sà-ji-gaa-yon
now	ตอนนี้	dtom níi
number	ตัวเลข	dtua lêek
phone number	หมายเลข	mãai lêek too-rá-
	โทรศัพท์	sàp
number plate	หมายเลข	mãai lêek tà-bian
	ทะเบียน	
nurse	พยาบาล	pa-yaa-baan
nuts (bar nibbles)	ถั่ว	tùa
O		
October	ตุลาคม	dtù-laa-kom
octopus	ปลาหมึกยักษ์	bplaa-mùk-yák
off (radio, engine)	ปิด	bpìd
this is off	มันเสีย	man sĭa
(milk, food)		
office	สำนักงาน	sãm-nák-ngaan
often	บ่อย	bò:i
oil	น้ำมัน	náam-man
OK	ตกลง	dtòk-long

English	Thai		English	Thai	
old	แก่	gàe	opening hours	ชั่วโมงทำการ	chûa-moong
how old is it?	มันอายุกี่ปี	man aa-yú kìi bpii?		ตรงข้าม	tam-gaan
(building, etc.)			opposite		drong-kâam
I'm ... years old...	ฉันอายุ ... ปี	chan aa-yú ... bpii	optician	หมอตา	mŏr dtaa
olives	มะกอก	má-gòrk	or	หรือ	rŭu
olive oil	น้ำมันมะกอก	náam-man má-gòrk	orange (colour)	สีส้ม	sĭi sôm
			orange	ส้ม	sôm
on	บน	bon	orange juice	น้ำส้ม	náam-sôm
		see GRAMMAR	to order (food)	สั่งอาหาร	sàng aa-hăan
once	ครั้งหนึ่ง	kráng nùng	other	อื่น อื่น	ùun ùun
at once	ทันที	tan-tii	our	ของเรา	kŏ:ng rao
one	หนึ่ง	nùng	out	ออก	òrk
onion	หัวหอมใหญ่	hŭa-hŏ:m-yài	out of order	ใช้การไม่ได้	chái gaan mâi dâai
only	เถาะนั้น	tâo nán	oven	เตาอบ	dtao-òp
only one	หนึ่งเดียวเถา	nùng diao tâo	to overtake	แซง	saeng
	นั้น	nán	to owe	ติดหนี้	dtìd-nîi
open	เปิด	bpèrd	you owe me...	คุณติดหนี้ฉัน...	Khun dtìd-nîi chan...
is it open?	มันเปิด	man bpèrd rĭu			
	หรือเปล่า?	bplàao?	owner	เจ้าของ	jâo-kŏ:ng
to open	เปิด	bpèrd			

P

P		
to pack (bags)	เก็บของใส่กระเป๋า	gèb kǒ:ng sài grà-bpǎo
package tour	ชุดโปรแกรมท่องเที่ยว	chút bproo-graem tô:ng-tîoa
packet	กระเป๋า	grà-bpǎo
paid	จ่าย	jàai
painful	เจ็บปวด	jèb bpùat
it's very painful	มันเจ็บปวดมาก	man bpùat mâak
painkiller	ยาแก้ปวด	yaa-gâe-bpùat
painting	ภาพวาด	pâap-wâad
(picture)		
pair	คู่	kûu
palace	วัง	wang
pancake	แพนเค้ก	paen-cake
paper	กระดาษ	grà-dàat
pardon!	ขอโทษครับ/ค่ะ	kǒr-tôot krab/kâ!
parents	พ่อแม่	pûu-bpòk-krong
park	สวน	sǔan

to park	จอด	jòrt
partner	หุ้นส่วน	hûn-sùan
(business)		
my partner	คู่ชีวิตของฉัน	kûu-chii-wìt kǒ:ng chan
(couple)		
party	ปาร์ตี้	bpaa-tîi
(celebration)		
passenger	ผู้โดยสาร	pûu-duoy-sǎan
passport	หนังสือเดินทาง	nǎng-sǔu-dum- taang
pasta	เพสต้า	pas-tâa
to pay	จ่าย	jàai
peanuts	ถั่ว	tùa
pearl	ไข่มุก	kài-múk
pedestrian	คนเดินเท้า	kon dum táao
pedestrian crossing	ทางข้าม	taang-kâam
pen	ปากกา	bpàak-gaa
pencil	ดินสอ	din-sǒr
penicillin	เพนนิซิลลิน	pen-ni-si-lin

English	Thai		English	Thai	
pepper (spice)	พริกไทย	prík-tai	**picture** (on wall)	ภาพ	pâap
per	ต่อ	dtòr	**pie**	พาย	paai
per hour	ต่อชั่วโมง	dtòr chûa-moong	**piece** (slice)	ชิ้น	chín
per week	ต่ออาทิตย์	dtòr aa-tít	**pill**	ยา	yaa
per kilometre	ต่อกิโลเมตร	dtòr gi-loo-met	**pillow**	หมอน	mŏrn
perfect	สมบูรณ์แบบ	sŏm-buun-bàep	**pin**	เข็ม	kĕm
it's perfect	มันสมบูรณ์แบบ	man sŏm-buun-bàep	**pink**	สีชมพู	sĭi-chom-puu
	แบบ		**pipe** (for smoking)	กล้องสูบยา	glôrng sùub yaa
performance	การแสดง	gaan sa-daeng	(drain, etc.)	ท่อน้ำ	tôr náam
perfume	น้ำหอม	náam hŏrm	**plain**	ธรรมดา	tii-râap
permit	อนุญาต	à-nú-yâat	**plane**	เครื่องบิน	krûang bin
person	บุคคล	bùk-kon	**plastic**	พลาสติก	plaas-tik
per person	ต่อคน	dtòr kon	**plate**	จาน	jaan
petrol	น้ำมันรถ	náam-man rót	**platform** (railway)	ชานชาลา	chaan-chaa-laa
petrol station	ปั๊มน้ำมัน	bpâm náam man	**to play**	เล่น	lên
phone	โทรศัพท์	too-rá-sàp	**please**	กรุณา	ga-ru-naa
phonecard	บัตรโทรศัพท์	bàt too-rá-sàp	**plug** (electric)	ปลั๊ก	bplák
photocopy	ใบสำเนา	bai-săm-nao	**plumber**	ช่างประปา	châang bprá-bpaa
photograph	ภาพถ่าย	pâap-tàai	**pocket**	กระเป๋าเสื้อ	grà-bpăo sûa
picnic	ปิกนิก	bpíc-nic	**poisonous**	เป็นพิษ	bpen pít

English – Thai

English	Thai	Pronunciation
police	ตำรวจ	dtam-rûat
police station	สถานีตำรวจ	sa-tăa-nii dtam-rûat
polish (for shoes)	ขัด	kàd
pool	สระน้ำ	sà-náam
is there a pool?	มีสระน้ำไหม?	mii sà-náam mái?
poor (not rich)	จน	jon
pork	หมูเนื้อ	nǔa-mŭu
port (harbour)	ท่าเรือ	tâa ruua
possible	เป็นไปได้	bpen bpai dâai
to post	ส่งทาง	sòng taang
	ไปรษณีย์	bprai-sa-nii
postbox	ตู้ไปรษณีย์	tôu-bprai-sa-nii
postcard	ไปรษณียบัตร	bprai-sa-nii-ya-bàt
postcode	รหัสไปรษณีย์	rà-hàt bprai-sa-nii
poster	โปสเตอร์	pos-sà-dtur
post office	ทำการ	tîi tam gaan
	ไปรษณีย์	bprai-sa-nii

English	Thai	Pronunciation
pot (for cooking)	หม้อ	môr
potato	มันฝรั่ง	man-fà-ràng
boiled potatoes	มันฝรั่งต้ม	man-fà-ràng-dtôm
fried potatoes	มันฝรั่งทอด	man-fà-ràng-tort
mashed potato	มันฝรั่งบด	man-fà-ràng-bòd
potato salad	สลัดมันฝรั่ง	sà-làd man-fà-ràng
powdered milk	นมผง	nom-pŏng
prawns	กุ้งใหญ่	gûng-yài
to prefer	ปรารถนา	bpràad-ta-nǎa
I'd prefer tea	ฉันต้องการชา	chan dtô:ng gaan chaa
pregnant	ท้อง	tórng
I'm pregnant	ฉันท้อง	chan tórng
prescription	ใบสั่งยา	bair-sàng yaa
present (gift)	ของขวัญ	kŏ:ng-kwǎn
this is a present	นี่คือของขวัญ	nîi kuu kŏ:ng-kwǎn
pretty	น่ารัก	nâa-rák

price	ราคา	raa-kaa
price list	ใบราคา	bai raa-kaa
private	ส่วนบุคคล	sùan bùk-kon
private bathroom	ห้องน้ำส่วนตัว	hôrng náam sùan-dtua
probably	คงจะ	kong jà
to pronounce	การออกเสียง	gaan òrk sĭang
public holiday	วันหยุดท้าวไป	wan yùt tûa-bpai
pudding	พุดดิ้ง	púd-dîng
purple	สีม่วง	sĭi mûang
to push	ผลัก	plàk
pushchair	รถเข็น	rót-kĕn
pyjamas	ชุดนอน	chút norn

Q

quality	คุณภาพ	kun-ná-pâap
good quality	คุณภาพดี	kun-ná-pâap dii
poor quality	คุณภาพไม่ดี	kun-ná-pâap mâi dii

queen	ราชินี	raa-chí-nii
question	คำถาม	kam-tăam
queue	คิว	kiw
to queue	เข้าคิว	kâo queue
quickly	อย่างเร็ว	yàang reo
quiet	เงียบ	ngîap
quilt	ผ้านวม	pâa-nuaam

R

rabbit (animal)	กระต่าย	grà-dtàai
rabies	โรคกลัวน้ำ	rôok-glua-náam
race (sport)	แข่ง	kàeng
radio	วิทยุ	wit-ta-yú
radish	หัวผักกาด	hŭa pàk-gàad
rain	ฝน	fŏn
raincoat	เสื้อกันฝน	sûa gan fŏn
raisins	ลูกเกด	lûuk gèet
rare (steak)	ดิบ	dìb
rash (skin)	ผื่น	pùun
rat	หนู	nŭu

English – Thai

rate	อัตรา	àt-dtraa
raw ham	แฮมดิบ	ham dìb
razor	มีดโกน	mîit-goon
to read (book, etc.)	อ่าน	àan
ready	พร้อม	prórm
is it ready?	มันพร้อมหรือยัง?	man prórm rǔu yang?
real	จริง, แท้	jing, táe
receipt	ใบเสร็จ	bai-sèt
reception (desk)	พนักงานตอนรับ	pa-nàk-ngaan dtôn-ráp
recipe	สูตรอาหาร	sùut aa-hǎan
to recommend	แนะนำ	náe-nam
red	สีแดง	sǐi daeng
red wine	ไวน์แดง	wine-deang
reduction	การลดลง	gaan lót long
to refund	คืนเงิน	kuun ngum
regulations	ระเบียบข้อบังคับ	ra-bìap kǒr bang-káp

relation (family member)	ความสัมพันธ์	kwaam-sǎm-pan
reliable (person, service)	เชื่อถือได้	chûa tǔu dâai
to remember	จำ	jam
rent	เช่า	cháo
to rent	การเช่า	gaan-cháo
to repair	การซ่อม	gaan-sôm
to repeat	การทำซ้ำ	gaan tam sám
reservation	การจอง	gaan jo:ng
to reserve (room, table, etc.)	จอง	jo:ng
reserved	จองแล้ว	jo:ng láew
to rest	พักผ่อน	pák-pòn
restaurant	ห้องอาหาร	hôŋ aa-hǎan
retired	เกษียณ	gà-sǐan
to return (ticket)	กลับ	glàb
return	ตั๋วกลับ	dtǔa glàb
reverse-charge call	เก็บเงินปลายทาง	gèb ngum bpaai taang

<table>
<tr><td>rice (cooked)</td><td>ข้าวสวย</td><td>kâao sŭay</td></tr>
<tr><td>rich (person)</td><td>รวย</td><td>ruai</td></tr>
<tr><td>right (correct)</td><td>ถูกต้อง</td><td>tùuk dtôːng</td></tr>
<tr><td>on/to the right</td><td>อยู่/ไปทางขวา</td><td>yùu/bpai taang kwǎa</td></tr>
<tr><td>ring (for finger)</td><td>แหวน</td><td>wǎen</td></tr>
<tr><td>river</td><td>แม่น้ำ</td><td>mâe náam</td></tr>
<tr><td>road</td><td>ถนน</td><td>tà-nŏn</td></tr>
<tr><td>road map</td><td>แผนที่ถนน</td><td>pǎen-tîi tà-nŏn</td></tr>
<tr><td>roof</td><td>หลังคา</td><td>lǎng-kaa</td></tr>
<tr><td>room</td><td>ห้อง</td><td>hôːng</td></tr>
<tr><td>rope</td><td>เชือก</td><td>chûak</td></tr>
<tr><td>rose</td><td>กุหลาบ</td><td>gù-làap</td></tr>
<tr><td>rotten (food)</td><td>เสีย</td><td>sĭa</td></tr>
<tr><td>route</td><td>เส้นทาง</td><td>sên-taang</td></tr>
<tr><td>rubber</td><td>ยาง</td><td>yaang</td></tr>
<tr><td>rug</td><td>พรม</td><td>prom</td></tr>
</table>

S

sad	เศร้า	sâo
safe (harmless)	เซฟ	séf
safe	ปลอดภัย	bplòrt-pai
safety pin	เข็มกลัด	kém glàd
sailing	ออกเรือ	òrk ruaa
sale	ขาย	kǎai
for sale	สำหรับขาย	sǎm-ráp kǎai
salad	สลัด	sà-làd
salesperson	พนักงานขาย	pa-nák-ngaan kǎai
salmon	ปลาแซลมอน	bplaa sael-mon
salt	เกลือ	glua
same	เหมือน	mǔan
sand	ทราย	saai
sandals	รองเท้าแตะ	roːng-táao dtàe
sardines	ปลาซาร์ดีน	bplaa-saa-diin
Saturday	วันเสาร์	wan sǎo
sauce	น้ำจิ้ม	náam jîm
sausage	ไส้กรอก	sài-gròrk

English	Thai	Transliteration
to say	พูด	pûud
school	โรงเรียน	roong-rian
scissors	กรรไกร	gan-grai
Scotland	สก็อตแลนด์	sà-gòt-laen
Scottish	คนสก็อตแลนด์	kon sà-gòt-laen
sculpture	แกะสลัก	chàang-bpàn
sea	ทะเล	tà-lee
seafood	อาหารทะเล	aa-hăan tá-lee
seasick	เมาเรือ	mao ruua
I'm feeling	จินเมาเรือ	chan mao ruua
seasick		
seat (chair)	ที่นั่ง	tîi nâng
reserved seat	ของที่นั่ง	jo·ng tîi nâng
seat belt	เข็มขัดนิรภัย	kĕm-kàt ni-ra-pai
second	วินาที	wínaa-tii
a second-class	ชั้นสอง	chán sŏ·ng
ticket	ตั๋วชั้นสอง	dtŭa chán sŏ·ng
secondhand	ของมือสอง	kŏ·ng muu sŏ·ng

English	Thai	Transliteration
to see	เห็น	hĕn
to sell	ขาย	kăai
to send	ส่ง	sòng
senior citizen	ผู้สูงอายุ	pûu sŭung aa-yú
separate	แยก	yâek
separately	แยกกัน	yâek gan
September	กันยายน	gan-yaa-yon
serious	จริงจัง	jing-jang
service	บริการ	bo·-ri-gaan
service charge	ค่าบริการ	kâa bo·-ri-gaan
shade (shadow)	เงามืด	rôm-ngao
shampoo	แชมพู	chaem-puu
to shave	โกน	goon
shaver	ที่โกนหนวด	tîi goon nùat
shaving cream	ครีมโกน	kriim-goon-nùat
	หนวด	
she	เธอ	tur
sheet (for bed)	ผ้าปูที่นอน	pâa–bpuu-dtiang
shelf	ชั้น	chán
shell	เปลือกหอย	bplùak-hŏ·i

English	Thai	
shellfish	หอย	hŏi
I don't eat shellfish	ฉันไม่กินหอย	chan mâi gin hŏi
ship	เรือ	ruua
shirt	เสื้อ	sûua
shoes	รองเท้า	ro:ng-táao
shop	ร้าน	ráan
shop assistant	พนักงานขาย	pa-nák-ngaan kăai
shopping	การเดินซื้อ	gaan dum súu
short	สั้น	kô:ng / sân
shorts (short trousers)	การเกงขาสั้น	gaang-geeng-kăa-sân
show	แสดง	sa-daeng
to show	การแสดง	gaan sa-daeng
shower (bath)	ฝักบัว	fàk bua
shrimps	กุ้ง	gûng
shut	ปิด	bpìd
to shut	การปิด	gaan bpìd

English	Thai	
sick	ป่วย	bpùai
I feel sick	ฉันรู้สึก คลื่นไส้	chan rúu-sùk klûun-sâi
sign (road, notice)	ป้าย	bpâai
to sign (form, cheque, etc.)	เซ็นชื่อ	sen chûu
signature	ลายเซ็น	laai-sen
silk	ไหม	măi
silver	เงิน	ngrn
simple	ธรรมดา	tam-má-daa
single (lone) (unmarried)	โสด	sòd
I'm single	ฉันเป็นคน โสด	chan bpen kon sòd
single room	ห้องเดี่ยว	hô:ng diao
sink	อ่างล้างจาน	àang láang jaan
sister (elder/ younger)	พี่สาว/ น้องสาว	pii-săao/ nó:ng-săao
sit	นั่ง	nâng

size (shoes)	ขนาด	kà-nàat
bigger size	ขนาดใหญ่	kà-nàat yài
smaller size	ขนาดเล็ก	kà-nàat lék
to skate	เล่นสเก็ต	lên sà-gét
skates	สเก็ต	sà-gét
skimmed milk	นมพร่องมันเนย	nom prôrng man neei
skin	ผิว	piu
skirt	กระโปรง	gra-bproong
sky	ท้องฟ้า	tórng fáa
to sleep	นอน	norn
sleeping bag	ถุงนอน	tǔng norn
sleeping pill	ยานอนหลับ	yaa-norn-làp
slice	ชิ้น	chín
slippers	รองเท้าแตะ	rorng-táao dtàe
slow	ช้า	cháa
small	เล็ก	lék
smaller	เล็กกว่า	lék gwàa
smell	กลิ่น	glìn
to smell	ได้กลิ่น	dâai glìn
smile	ยิ้ม	yím
smoke	ควัน	kwan
to smoke	สูบบุหรี่	sùub burìi
snake	งู	nguu
soap	สบู่	sà-bùu
socks	ถุงเท้า	tǔng-táao
soft	นิ่ม	nîm
soft drink	เครื่องดื่ม	krûang dùum
sold out	ขายออก	kǎai òrn
someone	บางคน	baang kon
something	บางอย่าง	baang yàang
sometimes	บางครั้ง	bang wee-laa
son	ลูกชาย	lûuk-chaai
song	เพลง	pleeng
soon	เร็วๆ นี้	reo reo níi
sorry:		
I'm sorry!	ขอโทษครับ / ค่ะ	kŏr-tôot kráb/ká
sort (type)	ชนิด	cha-nít

English			English		
soup	หม้งแกง	náam-gaeng	**to start**	เริ่ม	rûrm
south	ใต้	dtâi	**station**	สถานี	sà-tãa-nii
souvenir	ของฝาก	kö:ng fàak	**bus station**	สถานีรถเมย์	sà-tãa-nii kõn
souvenir shop	ร้านขายของ	rãan kãai kö:ng			sòng
	ฝาก	fàak	**railway station**	สถานีรถไฟ	sà-tãa-nii rót fai
to speak	พูด	pûud	**to stay**	พัก	pák
special	พิเศษ	pi-sèet	**still** (not fizzy)	ไม่ซ่า,	mái sâa,
speed	ความเร็ว	kwaam reo		ไม่มีฟอง	mái mii fo:ng
spell	สะกด	sà-kòt	**stomach**	ท้อง	tó:ng
spicy	เผ็ด	pèt	**stop!**	หยุด!	yùd!
sponge (for cleaning)	ฟองน้ำ	fo:ng-náam	**storm**	พายุ	paa-yú
			straight on	ตรงไป	dtrong bpai
spoon	ช้อน	chó:n	**straw** (for drinking)	หลอด	lòrdt
sport	กีฬา	gii-laa			
squid	ปลาหมึกตัว	bplaa-mùk dtua	**street**	ถนน	tà-nõn
	เล็ก	lék	**street map**	แผนที่ถนน	pàen-tîi tà-nõn
stadium	สนามกีฬา	sà-nãam gii-laa	**string**	ด้าย	dâai
stairs	บันได	ban-dai	**strong** (tea, coffee)	เข้ม	kêm
stamp	แสตมป์	sà-dtaem			
star	ดาว	dao			

English	Thai	Pronunciation
stuck:		
it's stuck	มันติด	man dtìd
student	เด็กนักเรียน	dèk nák rian
stupid	โง่	ngôe
sugar	น้ำตาล	náam dtaan
suit (clothes)	สูท	sùut
suitcase	กระเป๋าเสื้อผ้า	grà-bpǎo sûa-pâa
summer	หน้าร้อน	nâa rórm
in summer	ในหน้าร้อน	nai nâa rórm
sun	พระอาทิตย์	prá aa-tít
sunbathe	อาบแดด	àap dàet
sunburn	ผิวไหม้แดด	pǐu-mâi-dàet
Sunday	วันอาทิตย์	wan aa-tít
sunglasses	แว่นกันแดด	wâen-gan-dàet
sunshade	ที่บังแดด	tîi-bang-dàet
suntan lotion	ครีมกันแดด	kriim-gan-dàet
supermarket	ซุปเปอร์	sup-bpur-maa-
	มาร์เก็ต	gét
supplement	หเริม	sǔrm

English	Thai	Pronunciation
surfboard	กระดานโต้	grà-daan-dtôe
	คลื่น	klûun
surfing	โต้คลื่น	dtôe klûun
surname	นามสกุล	naam-sà-kun
sweater	เสื้อกันหนาว	sûa-gan-nǎao
sweetener	หวาน	wǎan
sweets	น้ำตาลเทียม	náam dtaan tiam
to swim	ว่ายน้ำ	wâai-náam
swimming-pool	สระว่ายน้ำ	sà wâai-náam
swimsuit	ชุดว่ายน้ำ	chút wâai-náam
switch	สวิทช์	sà-wít
to switch off	ปิด	bpìd
to switch on	เปิด	bpùrd
swollen (finger, ankle, etc.)	บวม	buam
T		
table	โต๊ะ	dtó
table tennis	ปิงปอง	bping-bpo:ng

English	Thai		English	Thai	
to take	กลาย	tàai	international	โทรศัพท์	too dtàang-bpra-
to talk	คุย	kui		ประเทศ	têet
tall	สูง	sŭung	call	สมุดโทรศัพท์	sà-mùt too-rá-
tap	เทน	tép			sàp
tape (cassette)	เทปคาสเส็ตต์	tép-ka-sèt	directory	โทรทัศน์	too-rá-tát
taste	รสชาติ	rót-châat	television	อุณหภูมิ	un-hà-puum
tasty	อร่อย	aròy	temperature	ฉันตัวร้อน	chan dtua rórn
tax	ภาษี	paa-sĭi	I have a		
taxi	แท็กซี่	táek-sîi	temporary	ชั่วคราว	chûa-kraao
tea	น้ำชา	náam-chaa	tennis	เทนนิส	ten-nís
teacher	ครู	kruu	tennis ball	ลูกเทนนิส	lûuk ten-nís
team (football, etc.)	ทีม	tiim	tennis court	สนามเทนนิส	sà-nǎam ten-nís
			tennis racket	ไม้เทนนิส	máai ten-nís
teeth	ฟัน	fan	tent	เต็นท์	dtén
telephone	โทรศัพท์	too-rá-sàp	terrace	ระเบียง	rá-biang
to telephone	โทร	too	tetanus	โรคบาดทะยัก	rôok-bàat-ta-yák
telephone box	ตู้โทรศัพท์	dtûu too-rá-sàp	thank you	ขอบคุณครับ /	kòrb kun krab/ká
telephone call	หมายเลขโทรศัพท์	mĭi too-rá-sàp		คะ	
		maa	thanks	ขอบใจ	kòrb jai
			that	นั่น	nán

English – Thai

theatre	โรงละคร	roong-la-korn
there:	ที่นั่น	tîi nân
there is…/ there are…	มี …	mii …
is there…?	มี … … ไหม?	mii … … mái?
these	เหล่านี้	lâo-níi
they	พวกเขา	pûag-kǎo
thief	โจร	kà-mooi
thin	ผอม	pǒrm
to think	คิด	kíd
I think so	ฉันเห็นด้วย	chan hěn dûoy
I don't think so	ฉันไม่เห็นด้วย	chan mâi hěn dûoy
thirsty:		
I'm thirsty	หิว (น้ำ), กระหาย	hiu (náam), gra-hǎai
this	ฉันหิวน้ำ นี้	chan hiu náam níi
those	เหล่านั้น	lâo-nán
thread	ด้าย	dâai

Thursday	วันพฤหัสบดี	wan-pá-rú-hàt-sa-bo:-dii
ticket	ตั๋ว	dtǔa
single ticket	ตั๋วเที่ยวเดียว	dtǔa tîao diao
return ticket	ตั๋วไปกลับ	dtǔa bpai glàb
ticket office	ที่ขายตั๋ว	tîi kǎai dtǔa
tie	เนคไท	neck-tai
tight	คับ	káb
it's too tight	มันคับจนเกินไป	man káb gum bpai
time	เวลา	wee-laa
timetable	ตารางเวลา	dtaa-raang wee-laa
tip (to waiter, etc.)	ทิป	tip
tired	เหนื่อย	nùai
tissues	ทิชชู่	tít-chûu
to	ไปที่	bpai tîi
		see GRAMMAR
to the station	ไปที่สถานี	bpai tîi sà-tǎa-nii
toast	ปิ้ง	bping
today	วันนี้	wan níi

English	Thai	
together	ด้วยกัน	dûay-gan
toilet	ห้องสุขา	hông su-kăa
toilet paper	กระดาษชำระ	grà-daat cham-rá
toll (on motorway)	ทางด่วน	taang dùan
tomato	มะเขือเทศ	má-kŭa-têet
tomato juice	น้ำมะเขือเทศ	náam má-kŭa-têet
tomato salad	สลัดมะเขือเทศ	sà-làd má-kŭa-têet
tomorrow	พรุ่งนี้, เมื่อพรุ่งนี้	prûng níi
tomorrow evening	เย็นพรุ่งนี้	yen prûng níi
tomorrow morning	พรุ่งนี้เช้า	prûng níi cháao
tonight	คืนนี้	kuun níi
tooth	ฟัน	fan
toothache	ปวดฟัน	bpùat-fan
toothbrush	แปรงสีฟัน	bpraeng sĭi-fan
toothpaste	ยาสีฟัน	yaa-sĭi-fan
total	รวมทั้งหมด	ruam táng mòt

English	Thai	
tough (meat)	เหนียว	nĭao
tour	ทัวร์	tuaa
tourist	นักท่องเที่ยว	nák-tô:ng-tîao
tourist office	สำนักบริการนักท่องเที่ยว	sŭun bo:-ri-gaan nák-tô:ng-tîao
towel (hand towel)	ผ้าเช็ดมือ	pâa chét muu
towel	ผ้าเช็ดตัว	pâa chét dtua
town	เมือง	muang
town hall	ศาลากลาง	săa-laa glaang
toy	ของเล่น	kŏ:ng lên
traditional	ตามประเพณี	dtaam bprà-pee-nii
traffic	จราจร	ja-raa-jorn
traffic lights	ไฟจราจร	fai ja-raa-jorn
train	รถไฟ	rót-fai
to translate	แปล	bplae
to travel	ท่องเที่ยว	tô:ng-tîao
travel agent	บริษัทท่องเที่ยว	bò:-ri-sàt tô:ng-tîao

travellers' cheques	เช็คเดินทาง	check-dum taang
tree	ต้นไม้	dtôn-máai
trip	การเดินทาง	gaan dum taang
trousers	กางเกงขายาว	gaang-geeng-kǎa-yao
truck	รถบรรทุก	rót-ban-túk
true	จริง	jing
that's true	มันจริง	man jing
that's not true	มันไม่จริง	man mâi jing
try on	ลองใส่	long sài
t-shirt	เสื้อยืด	sêua yûud
Tuesday	วันอังคาร	wan ang-kaan
tuna	ปลาทูน่า	bplaa-tuu-nâa
tunnel	อุโมงค์	ù-moong
to turn off (radio, light)	ปิด	bpìd
to turn on	เปิด	bpèrd
tweezers	คีมหนีบ	kiim-nîip
twins	ฝาแฝด	fǎa-fàet

U

ugly	น่าเกลียด	nâa-glìat
umbrella	ร่ม	rôm
uncle (paternal)	อา	aa
(maternal)	น้า	náa
uncomfortable	ไม่สะดวก	mâi sà-dùak
underground (metro)	รถไฟใต้ดิน	rót fai dâi din
understand	เข้าใจ	kâo jai
I don't understand	ฉันไม่เข้าใจ	chan mâi kâo jai
do you understand?	คุณเข้าใจไหม	khun kâo jai mái?
underwear	ชุดชั้นใน	chút chán nai
unemployed	ว่างงาน	wâang ngaan
university	มหาวิทยาลัย	má-hǎa-wít-ta-yaa-lai
unlucky	โชคร้าย	chôok-ráai
upstairs	ชั้นบน	chán bon
urgent	ด่วน	dùan

English	Thai	
it's urgent	มีเหตุด่วน	man dùan
to use	ใช้	chái
useful	มีประโยชน์	mii brà-yòot
usually	ปกติ	bpòk-gà-dti
V		
vacancy (room)	ห้องว่าง	hôrng wâang
vacuum cleaner	เครื่องดูดฝุ่น	krûeang dùut fùn
valid	ไม่หมดอายุ	mǎi mòt aa-yú
valuable	มีค่า	mii-kâa
van	รถตู้	rót dtûu
VAT	เงินมูลค่าเพิ่ม	paa-sǐi muun-la-kâa-pôem
veal	เนื้อลูกวัว	núea lûuk wua
vegetable	ผัก	pàk
vegetarian	มังสวิรัติ	mang sà-wí-rát
very	มาก	mâak
very good	ดีมาก	dii mâak
view	ดู	duu

English	Thai	
village	หมู่บ้าน	mùu-bâan
visa	วีซ่า	vii-sâa
to visit	เยี่ยม	yîam
vitamin pills	ผู้มาเยี่ยม	pûu maa yîam
volleyball	วิตามิน	vít-tà-min
	วอลเลย์บอล	vol-lêe-bo:n
W		
to wait (for)	รอ	ror
please wait	กรุณารอด้วย	ka-ru-naa ror
	ด้วย	pôm dôy
waiter/	พนักงานเสิร์ฟ	pa-nák-ngaan
waitress		sèrp
waiting room	ห้องนั่งรอ	hôrng nâng ror
to wake up	ตื่น	dtùun
walk	เดิน	durn
to walk	เดิน	durn
walking-stick	ไม้เท้า	máai táao
wallet	กระเป๋าเงิน	grà-bpǎo ngurn
to want	ต้องการ	dtôrng gaan

English – Thai

English	Thai	Pronunciation
war	สงคราม	sŏng-kraam
wardrobe	ตู้เสื้อผ้า	dtûu sûa-pâa
warm	อุ่น	ùn
to wash	ล้าง	láang
washbasin	อ่างล้างหน้า	àang láang nâa
washing machine	เครื่องซักผ้า	krûang sák pâa
washing powder	น้ำยาซักผ้า	náam yaa sák pâa
wasp	ตัวต่อ	dtua dtòr
watch (wrist)	นาฬิกาข้อมือ	naa-li-gaa kôr muu
water	น้ำ	náam
distilled water	น้ำกลั่น	náam glàn
mineral water	น้ำแร่	náam râe
fresh water	น้ำสะอาด	náam sà-àat
waterfall	น้ำตก	náam dtòk
waterproof	กันน้ำ	gan-náam
water-skiing	สกีน้ำ	sà-gii náam
wave	คลื่น	klûun
way	ทาง	taang
is this the right way?	ตรงนี้ถูกทางไหม	drong níi tùuk taang mái?
way out	ทางออก	taang òrk
we	เรา	rao
weak (tea, coffee, drink)		see GRAMMAR mâi kêm kôn
to wear	ใส่	sài
weather forecast	พยากรณ์อากาศ	pa-yaa-gorn aa-gàat
wedding	งานแต่งงาน	ngaan dtàeng-ngaan
wedding ring	แหวนแต่งงาน	wăen dtàeng-ngaan
Wednesday	วันพุธ	wan pút
week	สัปดาห์	sàp-daa
last week	สัปดาห์ที่แล้ว	sàp-daa tîi láew
next week	สัปดาห์หน้า	sàp-daa nâa

English	Thai	
weekend	วันหยุดเสาร์อาทิตย์	wan-yùd sǎo aa-tít
weekly	ประจำสัปดาห์	bpra-jam sàp-daa
weight	น้ำหนัก	náam-nàk
welcome!	ยินดีต้อนรับ!	Yindii dtôːn ráb!
well	ดี	dii
well done (meat)	สุกสุก	sùk sùk
west	ตะวันตก	dtà wan dtòk
wet	เปียก	bpiak
what	อะไร	a-rai
what is it?	มันคืออะไร	man kuu a-rai?
wheelchair	รถเข็น	rót kén
when?	เมื่อไหร่	mûa-rài?
where?	ที่ไหน	tîi nǎi?
which?	อันไหน	an nǎi?
which one?	อันไหน	an nǎi?
white	ขาว	kǎo
who	ใคร	krai
whole	ทั้งหมด	táng mòt

English	Thai	
whose:	ของใคร	kǒːng krai
whose is it?	มันเป็นของใคร?	man bpen kǒːng krai?
why	ทำไม	tam-mai
wife	ภรรยา	panrayaa
window	หน้าต่าง	nâa-dtàang
windy:	ลมแรง	lom raeng
it's windy	ลมแรง	lom raeng
wine	ไวน์	wine
red wine	ไวน์แดง	wine-daeng
white wine	ไวน์ขาว	wine-kǎo
wine list	รายการไวน์	raai gaan wine
with	ด้วย	dûay
without	ปราศจาก	bpràat-sa-jàak
woman	ผู้หญิง	see GRAMMAR / pûu-yǐng
wood (substance)	แผ่นไม้	pàen mái
word	คำ	kam
to work	ทำงาน	tam-ngaan

English – Thai

it doesn't work	มันไม่ทำงาน	man mâi tam-ngaan
wrap	ห่อ	hòr
please wrap it up	ช่วยห่อให้มันด้วยครับ / คะ	chûai hòr man dûoy krab/kà
to write	เขียน	kian
writing paper	กระดาษ	grà-dàat
wrong	ผิด	pìd

X

| x-ray | เอ็กซ์เรย์ | ék-sà-ree |

Y

yacht	เรือยอชต์	ruua yórt
year	ปี	bpii
this year	ปีนี้	bpii níi
yellow	สีเหลือง	sĭi lŭang
yes	ใช่	châi
yesterday	เมื่อวาน	mûa-waan
you	คุณ	khun

Z

zero	ศูนย์	sŭun
zip code	รหัสฯไปรษณีย์	rá-hàt-prai-sa-nii
zoo	สวนสัตว์	sŭan sàt

Thai – English

ก		
กระเป๋าเข็มขัด	grà-bpăo kěm-kàt	money belt
การเข้าไป	gaan kâo bpai	to enter
กระเป๋าเสื้อ	grà-bpăo sûa	pocket
กระดาษ	grà-dàat	paper
กระต่าย	grà-dtàai	rabbit (animal)
กรุณาอย่าสูบบุหรี่	ga-ru-naa yàa sùub burìi	please don't smoke
กลับไป	glàb bpai	to go back
ก่อนอาหารค่ำ	gòn aa-hăan kâm	before dinner
กางเกงยีนส์	gaang-geeng-kăa-yao	trousers
การหลบหนี	gaan lòp nĩi	escape
กุมภาพันธ์	gum-paa-pan	February
เก็บเงินทอนไว้ครับ/ค่ะ	gèb ngurn torn wái krab/ká	keep the change
เกาะ	gò	island
กรมท่า	grom-mà-tâa	navy blue
กรรไกร	gan-grai	scissors
กระดาษชำระ	grà-dàat cham-rá	toilet paper
การอธิบาย	ka-ru-naa à-tí-baai	please explain
กล่อง	glò:ng	box
กลุ่ม	glùm	group (of people)
ก่อนหน้า	gò:n nâa	before
ก่อนสี่โมง	gò:n sìi moong	before 4 o'clock
กอล์ฟ	golf	golf
กาแฟเย็น	gaa-fae-yen	iced coffee
กาแฟสำเร็จรูป	gaa-fae săm-rèt-rûub	instant coffee
การจอง	gaan jorng	booking
การตัด	dtàt	to cut
การประชุม	gaan bpra-chum	meeting
กิน	gin	to eat
กุ้งย่าง	gûng-yâl	prawns
เก็บเงินด้วยครับ/ค่ะ	gèb ngurn dûoy krab/ká	the bill, please
เก็บเงินทอนไว้ครับ/ค่ะ	gèb ngurn torn wái krab/ká	keep the change

เก็บเงินปลาย	gèb ngurn bplaai	reverse-charge
ทาง	taang	call
เกมส์	game	match (game)
เกลือ	glua	salt
เก็บ	gèb	to keep
เก้าอี้	gâo-îi	chair
เก้าอี้ผ้าใบ	gâo-îi-pâa-bai	deck chair
เกาะไอร์	gò: ai-laen nûa	Northern Ireland
แลนด์เหนือ		
เกิดขึ้น	gùrt kûn	to happen
แก้ไร	gùrt a-rai kûn?	what happened?
กรกฎาคม	gas	gas
	gà-rá-gà-daa-kom	July
กระเทียม	grà-tiam	garlic
กระเป๋า	grà-bpǎo	pocket
กระเป๋า	grà-bpǎo	bag
กระเป๋าเดินทาง	grà-bpǎo durn taang	baggage

กระเป๋า	grà-bpǎo durn taang	luggage
กระเป๋าใส่เสื้อผ้า	grà-bpǎo sûa-pâa	suitcase
กระเป๋าถือ	grà-bpǎo tǔu	hand luggage
กระเป๋ามือถือ	grà-bpǎo muu tǔu	handbag
กระแสไฟ	grà-sǎe-fai	current
กระโปรงชุด	grà-bproong-chút	dress
กระจก	grà-jòk	mirror
กระดานโต้	grà-daan-dtôo klûun	surfboard
คลื่น		
กระดาษ	grà-dàat	writing paper
กระดูก	grà-dùuk	bone
กระป๋อง	grà-bpǒng	can
กระปุก	grà-bpùk	jar
ก้ม	gôm	bend
กล้องถ่ายรูป	glô:ng tàai rûub	camera
กล้องถ่ายภาพ	glô:ng tàai nǎng	camcorder
เคลื่อนไหว		
กลาง	glaang	middle
กลางคืน	glaang kuun	night
กอล์ฟคลับ	golf club	golf club

Thai – English

Thai – English

Thai	Transcription	English
กัด	gàt	bite (insect, dog)
กันน้ำ	gan-náam	waterproof
กาแฟ	gaa-fae	coffee
กาแฟที่ไม่มีกาเฟอีน	gaa-fae mâi mii kaa-fee-in	decaffeinated coffee
กาแฟดำ	gaa-fae-dam	black coffee
กาแฟสำเร็จรูป	gaa-fae săm-rèt-rûub	instant coffee
กางเกงขายาว	gaang-geeng-kăa-yao	pants (trousers)
กางเกงขาสั้น	gaang-geeng-kăa-sân	shorts (shorts)
การเต้นรำ	gaan dtên-ram	dance
การเข้าไปสู่	gaan kâo bpai súu	to get into
การเช่า	gaan châo	to rent
การเดินซื้อของ	gaan dum súu kŏ:ng	shopping
การเปิด	gaan bpùrd	open
การแสดง	gaan sa-daeng	to show
การแสดง	gaan sa-daeng	performance
การควบคุมอาหาร	gaan kûap-kum aa-hăan	diet
การซ่อม	gaan sô:m	to repair
การ์ด	gáat	card
การ์ดวันเกิด	gáat wan gùrt	birthday card
การดื่ม	gaan dùum	to drink
การบันเทิง	gaan ban-tung	entertainment
การบิน	gaan bin	fly
การปิด	gaan bpìd	to shut
การออกเสียง	gaan òk sĭang	pronunciation
การอาบน้ำ	gaan-àap-náam	bath
กีฬา	gii-laa	game (sport)
เกษียณ	gà-sĭan	retired
แก่	gàe	old
กระเป๋าเงิน	grà-bpăo ngurn	wallet
กระโปรง	gra-proong	skirt
กรุณา	ga-ru-naa	please
กลิ่น	glìn	smell
กันยายน	gan-yaa-yon	September
การเชิญ	gaan churn	to invite

Thai – English

เข็มกับด้าย	kěm gàb dâai	a needle and thread
เข็มทิศ	kěm-tít	compass
เขา	kǎo	he
เข้าใจ	kâo jai	understand
เข้าไป	kâo bpai	to go in
เข้ามา	kâo-maa	come in!
เขียน	kian	to write
เขียว	kiao	green
แข่ง	kàeng	race (sport)
ขนาดเล็ก	kà-nàat lék	small size
ขม	kŏm	bitter (taste)
ขวด	kùat	bottle
ขอโทษ	kŏr-tôot!	pardon!
ขนมปัง	ka-nŏm bpang	bread
ขนาด	kà-nàat	size (shoes)
ขนาดใหญ่	kà-nàat yài	bigger size
ขยะ	kà-yà	litter (rubbish)
ของใคร	kŏrng krai	whose
ของฝาก	kŏrng fàak	souvenir

Thai – English

ข้างหน้า	kang nar	front
ข้างหน้า	kâang nâa	straight ahead
ขาย	kǎai	to sell
ขาว	kǎao	white
ไข่	kài	egg
ไข่มุก	kài-múk	pearl
ขอโทษครับ/ค่ะ!	kŏr tôot krab/kâ!	I'm sorry!
ข้อความ	kôr-kwaam	message
ของเล่น	kŏ:ng lên	toy
ของมือสอง	kŏ:ng muu sŏ:ng	secondhand
ของหวาน	kŏ:ng-wăan	dessert
ขอบคุณครับ/ค่ะ	kòrb kun krab/ká	thank you
ขัด	kàd	polish (for shoes)
ข้อมูล	kôr-moon	information
ขับ	kàp	to drive
ขา	kăa	leg
ขาเข้า	kăa-kâo	arrivals
ข้างบน	kâang-bon	above

Thai	Phonetic	English
ข้างหน้า	kâang nâa	in front of
ข้างหลัง	kâang lăng	behind
ขาย	kăai	sale, for sale
ขายหมด	kăai mòt	sold out
ข่าว	kàao	news
ข้าวสวย	kâao sŭay	rice (cooked)
ไข้หวัดใหญ่	kâi-wàt-yài	flu
คง		
คงจะ	kong jà	probably
คนเดินถนน	kon dun tăao	pedestrian
คนขับ	kon kàp	driver
คนดูแลเด็ก	kon-duu-lae-dèk	baby-sitter
คนฝรั่งเศส	kon fa-ràng-sèet	French
คนพิการ	kon pí-gaan	disabled (person)
คนรับใช้	kon ráp chái	maid
คนสก็อตแลนด์	kon sà-gó:t-laen	Scottish
ค้นหา	kón-hăa	to find
คนอังกฤษ	kon ang-grìt	English
ครอบครัว	krôrp-krua	family

Thai	Phonetic	English
ครั้งแรก	kráng râek	first
ครีมกันแดด	kriim-gan-dàet	suntan lotion
ครีมนวดผม	kriim-nûat-pŏm	conditioner (for hair)
คีมหนีบ	kiim-nìp	tweezers
ครึ่งชั่วโมง	krûng chûa moong	half an hour
คลื่น	klûun	wave
ควัน	kwan	smoke
ความเร็ว	kwaam-reo	speed
ความดันโลหิต	kwaam-dan-lôat	blood pressure
ความดันสูง	kwaam-dan-sŭung	high blood pressure
ความสนใจ	kwaam-sŏn-jai	attention
ความสัมพันธ์	kwaam-săm-pan	relation (family member)
ความสูง	kwaam-sŭung	height
อันตราย	an-dta-raai	danger
คอนแท็คเลนส์	ko:n-tàek-len	contact lens
คอมพิวเตอร์	com-pu-ter	computer
เครดิตการ์ด	kree-dìt-gàat	credit card

Thai – English

เครื่องดื่มมึนเมา – คุณชื่ออะไร

เครื่องดื่ม มึนเมา	krûang dùum mun-mao	alcohol
เค้ก	kâyk	cake
คริสต์มาส	krít-sà-mâat	Christmas
คนเยอรมัน	kon yur-rà-man	German
ครอบครัวฉัน	krôp-krua kŏ:ng chan	my family
คอ	kor	neck
ค่าโดยสาร	kâa duoy-săan	fare (train, bus)
คุณสบายดีหรือ	khun sà baai dii rúu?	how are you?
โค้ก	kôok	Coke®
โคมไฟ	koom-fai	lamp
คนจับปลา	kon jàb bplaa	fisherman
คนต่างชาติ	kon dtàang-châat	foreigner
คนทำขนมปัง	kon tam ka-nŏm bpang	baker's
คนออสเตรเลีย	kon ò:t-sa-dtree-lia	Australian
คนอิตาลี	kon ì-dtaa-lii	Italian

ครีม	kriim	cream (dairy)
ครึ่ง	krûng	half
ครึ่งขวด	krûng kùat	half bottle
ครู	kruu	teacher
ความเร็วสูงสุด	kwaam-reo sŭung sùt	maximum speed
ความถี่	kwaam tìi	frequency
ความร้อน	kwaam rórn	heat
ความสะอาด	kwaam sà-àat	cleanliness
ความสุข	kwaam sùk	happiness
ผ้าฝ้าย	kó:t-dtò:n, pâa fâai	cotton (material)
คอนเสิร์ต	kon-sùrt	concert
ค่าเข้า	kâa kâo	entrance fee
ค่าธรรมเนียม	kâa-tam-niam	charge (fee)
คำ	kam	word
คำตอบ	kam-dtorb	answer
คุณชื่ออะไร?	khun chûu a-rai?	what's your name?
ใคร	krai	who

คู่ชีวิตของฉัน	kûu-chii-wít	my partner
	kô:ng chan	(couple)
เคมี	kee-mii	chemistry
เครื่องดูดฝุ่น	krûang dùut fun	vacuum cleaner
เครื่องบิน	krûang bin	aeroplane, plane
เครื่องประดับ	krûang bprà dàb	jewellery
เคาน์เตอร์	káo-dtur	counter
แคบ	kâep	narrow
คัน	kan	itch
คับ	káb	tight
มันคับกุมไป	man káb gum bpai	it's too tight
ค่าธรรมเนียม	kâa-tam-niam	service charge
ค่าบริการ	kâa bo:-rí-gaan	fee
ค่าปรับ	kâa bpràp	fine (to be paid)
คิด	kíd	to think
คืนนี้	kuun níi	tonight
คุณ	khun	you
คุณภาพ	kun-nà-pâap	quality
คุณภาพไม่ดี	kun-nà-pâap mâi dii	poor quality

คุณภาพดี	kun-nà-pâap dii	good quality
คุย	kui	to talk
คู่	kûu	pair
คู่หมั้น	kûu mân	fiancé(e)
เครื่องยนต์	krûang-yon	engine
เครื่องซักผ้า	krûang sák pâa	washing machine
คนขายเนื้อ	kon kăai núa	butcher's
คนทำอาหาร	kon tam aa-hăan	a cook
คนอเมริกา	kon a-mee-rí-gaa	American
ครั้งหนึ่ง	kráng nùng	once
ทันที	tan-tii	at once
ครีมโกนหนวด	kriim-goon-nùat	shaving cream
เครื่องดื่ม	krûang dùum	soft drink
อย่างอ่อน	yaang òrn	
คำถาม	kam tăam	question
คืนเงิน	kuun ngurn	refund
คุณติดหนี้ฉัน	khun dtìd-nìi chan	you owe me...

Thai – English

Thai – English

ง

เงิน	ngrm	money
เงิน	ngrm	silver
งาน	ngaan	job
งู	nguu	snake
เงินสด	ngrm-sòt	cash
เงียบ	ngîap	quiet
งานแต่งงาน	ngaan dtàeng-ngaan	wedding

จ

จบ	jòb	end
จำนวนเท่าไร	jam-nuan tâo-rài?	how many?
จมน้ำ	jom náam	to drown
จมูก	jà-mùuk	nose
จราจร	ja-raa-jom	traffic
จอง	jo:ng	to queue to book
จองที่นั่ง	jo:ng tîi nâng	to reserve a seat
จอด	jòrt	land
จักรยาน	jàk-grà-yaan	bicycle
จาก	jàak	to leave

จาก	jàak	from
จากไป	jàak bpai	go away
จ่าย	jàai	to pay
จำเป็น	jam-bpen	necessary
จูบ	jùup	to kiss
เจ็บ	jèb	hurt
เจ้าของ	jâo-kǒ:ng	owner
จน	jon	poor (not rich)
เจ็บปวด	jèb bpùat	painful
โจมตี/ ประจัญ	joom-dtii (war)/ bpra-tùt-sa-ráai	to attack (person)
ใจดี	jai dii	kind
คุณใจดีมาก	khun jai dii mâak	you're very kind
จำนวน	jam-nuan	amount
จ่าย	jàai	to pay
จาน	jaan	plate
จะซื้อ	jà súu	to buy
จอง	jo:ng	to reserve (room, table, etc.)
จองแล้ว	jo:ng láew	reserved

Thai		English
จริงจังหรือ	jing-jang rúu?	is it serious?
จริงจัง	jing-jang	serious
จริง	jing	true
จริง	jing	real
จู่โจม/ทำร้าย	jùu-joom/ gam-rúrp	attack
จำ	jam	to remember
จะบิน	jà bin	to fly
จอด	jòrt	to park
ฉันเจ็บมือ	chan jèb muu	my hand hurts
ฉันเป็นคนโสด	chan bpen kon sòod	I'm single
ฉันเป็นคนอังกฤษ	chan bpen kon ang-grìt	I'm English
ฉันเห็นด้วย	chan hén dûoy	I think so
ฉันเหนื่อย	chan nùai	I feel tired
ฉันแต่งงานแล้ว	chan dàeng-ngaan láew	I'm married
ฉันชื่อ	chan chûu	my name is

Thai		English
ฉัน	chan	I
ฉันไม่เข้าใจ	chan mâi kâo jai	I don't understand
ฉันท้อง	chan tórng	I'm pregnant
ฉันต้องการ	chan dtô:ng gaan	I need...
ฉันต้องไป	chan dtô:ng bpai	I need to go
ฉันชอบ	chan chôrp	I like coffee
กาแฟ	gaa-fae	
ฉันจองไว้แล้ว	chan jo:ng wai láew	I've booked
ฉันไม่ชอบ	chan mâi chôrp	I don't like
กาแฟ	gaa-fae	coffee
ฉันไม่คิดว่า	chan mâi hén dûoy	I don't think so
ฉันโกรธ	chan gròot	I'm angry
ฉันเมา	chan mao	I'm drunk
ฉันเป็นหม้าย	chan bpen mâai	I'm divorced
ฉันเป็นโสด	chan bpen sòod	I'm not married
ฉันไม่เป็นไรอะไร	chan mâi bpen a-rai	I'm all right

Thai – English

ฉันไม่รู้	chan mâi rúu	I don't know
ฉันตัวร้อน	chan dtua rórm	I have a temperature
ฉันถ่ายภาพ	chan tàai-pâap	can I take
ได้ไหม	dâai măi	pictures?
ฉันปวดหัว	chan bpùat hŭa	I've got a headache
ฉันป่วย	chan bpùai	I'm ill
ฉันรักคุณ	chan rák khun	I love you
เช็คอิน	check-in	to check in
ชน	chon	crash (collision)
ช็อกโกแลต	chók-goo-làet	chocolate
ชอบ	chôp	enjoy
ชั้นบน	chán bon	upstairs
ชั้นสอง	chán sŏng	second-class
ชั้นหนึ่ง	chán nùng	first floor
ชั้นหนึ่ง	chán nùng	first class
ชั่วโมง	chûa-moong	hour

Thai – English

ชั่วโมงทำการ	chûa-moong tam gaan	opening hours
ชั่วคราว	chûa-kraao	temporary
ช้า	cháa	slow
ช่างทำผม	châang tam pŏm	hairdresser
ชานเมือง	chaan muang	suburb
ช่างปั้น	châang-bpân	sculpture
เช็ค	check	cheque
เช็คเดินทาง	check-dum-taang	travellers' cheques
เฌอรี่	chur-rîi	cherry
เช่า	châo	to hire
เช้านี้	cháao níi	this morning
เชือก	chûak	rope
แช่แข็ง	châe-kăeng	frozen
แชมเปญ	chaem-bpeen	champagne
แชมพู	chaem-puu	shampoo
โชคร้าย	chôok-ráai	unlucky
ใช่	châi	yes
ใช้	chái	to use

Thai		English
ไชโย	chai-yo	cheers!
ชิ้น	chín	piece (slice)
ชุดโปรแกรมท่องเที่ยว	chút bproo-graem tôːng-tîao	package tour
ชุดนอน	chút norn	pyjamas
เช่า	châo	rent
เชื่อถือได้	chûa tǔu dâai	reliable (person, service)
ชุดชั้นใน	chút chán nai	underwear
ชื่อ	chûu	name
ชิ้น	chín	slice
ชานชาลาไหน	chaan-chaa-laa nái?	which platform?
ชานชาลา	chaan-chaa-laa	platform (railway)
ชั้น	chán	shelf
ช้อน	chóːn	spoon
ช็อกโกแล็ตร้อน	chóːk-goo-lǽt rórn	hot chocolate
สีชมพู	sǐr-chom-puu	pink
ชนบท	chon-ná-bòt	country side

Thai		English
ชุดว่ายน้ำ	chút wâai-náam	swimsuit
ชีส	chíi	cheese
ชาวนา	chao naa	farmer
ชายหาด	chaai-hàat	beach
ชาดำเย็น	chaa-dam-yen	iced coffee
ช่างประปา	châang bpra-bpaa	plumber
ช่างตัดผม	châang-dàt-pǒm	barber
ชาเย็น	chaa-yen	iced tea
ชั้นล่าง	chán lâang	downstairs
ชั้น	chán	floor
ชอบ	chôrp	to like
ช่องแช่เย็น	chôːng-chɛ̂ɛ-yen	freezer
ช่วยด้วย	chûai dûay	help!
ช่วย	chûai	to help
ช่วงบ่ายนี้	chûang bàai níi	in the afternoon
เช็ค	cheque	cheque
เช้าเช้า	cháo cháao	early
เชื่อ	chûa	to believe
เชื้อเพลิง	chúa plœːng	fuel

Thai – English

ฬ		
เช้นชื่อ	sen chûu	to sign (form, cheque, etc.)
ซิการ์	sí-gǎa	cigar
ซีดี	sii-dii	CD
ซุปเปอร์	súp-bpôr-maa-	supermarket
มาร์เก็ต	gèt	
แซลมอน	saen-môːn	salmon
ซ่อม	sôːm	fix
เซฟ	sêf	safe
ซองจดหมาย	soːng-jòt- mǎai	envelope
ญาติ	yâat	relative
ฐ		
ฐานะ	tǎa-ná	position, status
เฒ่า	tâo	very old person
ณ		
เณร	neen	Buddhist novice

ด		
ดูแล	duu-lae	to look after
ดึง	dung	someone
		to pull
เด็กผู้ชาย	dèk pûu chaai	boy
ดาว	daao	star
ด้าย	dâai	thread
ดาย	daai	string
ดัง	dang	loud
ดี	dii	well
ได้กลิ่น	dâai glìn	to smell
ดีที่สุด	dii-tîi-sùt	the best
โดยรถไฟ	duoy-rót-fai	by train
โดยทันที	duoy tan-tii	immediately
โดยรถบัส	duoy rót-bus	by bus
ด้วย	dûoy	with
ด้วยกัน	dûoy-gan	together
ด่านศุลกากร	dàan sǔn-lá-gaa- gorn	customs control

Thai – English

Thai	Romanization	English
ดำน้ำ	dam náam	to dive
ดี	dii	good
ดื่ม	dùum	drink
เด็ก	dèk	child
เด็กนักเรียน	dèk nák rian	student
เดิน	dəən	to walk
เดือน	duan	month
ตุลาคม	dtù-laa-kom	October
ตั๋วชั้นสอง	dtŭa chán sŏng	a second-class ticket
ตั๋วไปกลับ	dtŭa bpai glàb	return (ticket)
ต่อกิโลเมตร	dtòr gi-loo-met	per kilometre
ต้นไม้	dtôn-máai	tree
ตกลง	dtòk-long	OK
ใต้	dtâi	south
เตียงคู่	dtiang kûu	double bed
ตอนเย็น	dtom yen	evening
ตู้โทรศัพท์	dtûu too-rá-sàp	telephone box
ตกลงไหม	dtòk-long mǎi	all right (OK)?
ตรงไปตี้	dtrong bpai-tîi	straight on
ตลอดไป	dta-lòrd bpai	always
ตลอดไป	dta-lòrd bpai	forever
ต่อคน	dtòr kon	per person
ต้องห้าม	dtôi ng hàam	forbidden
ต่อชั่วโมง	dtòr chûamoong	per hour
ตอนเช้า	dtorn cháao	morning
ตอบ	dtorb	to answer
ต่อรอง	dtòr rorg	bargain
ตะกร้า	dtà-grâa	basket
ตะวันตก	dtà wan dtòk	west
ตัด	dtàt	cut
ตัดผม	dtàt-pŏm	haircut
ตัน	dtan	blocked
ตัวแทน	dtua taen	agent
ตั๋วไปกลับ	dtŭa bpai glàb	return ticket
ตั๋วเที่ยวเดียว	dtŭa tîao diao	single ticket
ตา	dtaa	eye
ตาบอด	dtaa-bòrt	blind (person)
ตาม	dtaam	to follow

Thai – English

Thai	Transliteration	English
ติดแสตมป์	dtìd sà-dtaem	to put a stamp on (an envelope)
ติดต่อสอบถาม	dtìd-dtòr sòrb-tǎam	enquiry desk
ติดต่อสอบถาม	dtìd-dtòr sòrb-tǎam	information office
น่าตื่นเต้น	nâa-dtùun-dtên	exciting
ตุ๊กตา	dtúk-gà-dtaa	doll
ตู้เย็น	dtûu-yen	fridge
ตู้ไปรษณีย์	dtûu prai-sa-nii	postbox
ตก	dtòk	to fall
ตกปลา	dtòk bplaa	to fish
ต้ม	dtôm	boiled (food)
ตรง	dtrong	direct
ตลาดนัด	dtà-làat-nát	bazaar, an open market
ต่อ	dtòr	per
ต่อ	dtòr	connection (train, plane)
ต่อไป	dtòr bpai	next
ต้องการ	dtô:ng gaan	to need
ต้องการ	dtô:ng gaan	to want
ตอนนี้	dtro:n níi	now
ต่อย	dtò:i	sting
ต่อว่า	dtòr-wâa	complain
ตะปู	dtà-bpuu	nail (metal)
ตะวันออก	dtà-wan-òrk	east
ตั๋ว	dtǔa	ticket
ตัวเลข	dtua lêek	number
ตัวต่อ	dtua dtòr	wasp
ตารางเวลา	dtaa-raang wee-laa	timetable
ตารางการบิน	dtaa-raang gaan bin	flight
ตำรวจ	dtam-rûat	police
ตำรวจดับเพลิง	dtam-rûat dàp-plrung	firemen
ติดหนี้	dtìd-nîi	to owe
ตื่น	dtùun	to wake up
ตู้เสื้อผ้า	dtûu sûa-pâa	wardrobe

Thai		English
เติม	dtem	full
แตงกวา	dtaeng-gwaa	cucumber
โต๊ะ	dtó	table
โต๊ะสำหรับเด็ก	dtó sǎm-ràp dèk	high chair
เต็นท์	dtén	tent
เตาอบ	dtao-òp	oven
เติม	dturm	to fill (up)
เตียงคู่	dtiang kûu	double bed
เตียงเดี่ยวคู่	dtiang diao kûu	twin beds
เตียง	dtiang	bed
เต้นรำ	dtên-ram	to dance
โต้คลื่น	dtôo klɨ̂un	surfing
โต๊ะเก็บเงิน	dtó gèb ngum	cash desk
ถั่วลิสง	tùa-lí-sŏng	peanuts
ถังน้ำ	tǎng náam	bucket
ถนน	tà-nŏn	street
ถั่ว	tùa	nuts

ท		
ทุกทุก	túk túk	every
ที่โกนหนวด	tîi goon nùat	shaver
ที่นั่ง	tîi nâng	seat, chair (on bus, train, etc.)
ที่เปิดไวน์	tîi bpùrd wine	corkscrew
ทิ้ง	tíng	left
ทำ	tam	to make
ทั้งหมด	táng-mòt	whole
ท้องฟ้า	tó:ng fáa	sky
ท่องเที่ยว	tô:ng-tîao	to travel
น้ำท่วม	náam-tûam	flood
ทราย	saai	sand
เทนนิส	ten-nís	tennis
เทป	téep	tape
เท่าไหร่	tâo-rài?	how much?
เท่านั้น	tâo nán	only
เที่ยงวัน	tîang-wan	midday
ทดแทน	tót-taen	to compensate, to replace

Thai – English

หมวย	tá-naai	lawyer
ทอง	torng	gold
ท้อง	tórng	pregnant
ท้อง	tórng	stomach
ทอด	tôrt	fried (food)
ท่อน้ำ	tôr náam	drain (etc.)
ทั้งหมด	táng-mòt	all
ท่าเรือ	tâa ruua	port (harbour)
ทาง	taang	way
ทางข้าม	taang-kâam	pedestrian crossing
ทางด่วน	taang dùan	motorway
ทางด่วน	taang dùan	toll (on motorway)
ทางออก	taang òrk	way out
ทางเข้า	taang kâo	entrance
ทางหนีไฟ	taang nii fai	fire exit
ทางออก	taang òrk	exit
ทางออกฉุกเฉิน	taang òrk chùk-chĕun	emergency exit

ทำให้แห้ง	tam-hâi-hâeng	to dry
ทำการล็อค	tam gaan lock	to lock
ทำความสะอาด	tam kwaam sà-àat	to clean
ทำงาน	tam ngaan	to work
ทำด้วยมือ	tam dûoy muu	hand-made
ทำอาหาร	tam aa-hăan	to cook
ทำไม	tam-mai	why
ทิชชู่	tít-chûu	tissues
ทิป	tip	tip (to waiter, etc.)
ที่	tîi	at
ที่เขี่ยบุหรี่	tîi kìa burìi	ashtray
ที่เปิดกระป๋อง	tîi bpèrd grà-bpŏng	can-opener
ที่แปรงผม	tîi bpraeng pŏm	hairbrush
ที่โชว์สินค้า	tîi show sìn-káa	boots
ที่ไหน	tîi năi	where?
ที่กรอง	tîi grong	filter
ที่กันแสง	tîi-gan-săeng	blinds (on window)
ที่ขายตั๋ว	tîi kăai dtŭa	ticket office

Thai	Transliteration	English
ห้องตดต	tîi dtìd-dtòr sǎm-	left-luggage
สัมภาระขาเข้า	paa-rá hǎai	office
ทำการไปรษณีย์	tîi tam gaan prai-	post office
	sa-nii	
บ้านวีผม	tîi wǐi pǒm	hairbrush
ที่นั่งเด็ก	tîi nâng dek	car seat (for child)
ที่นั่น	tîi nân	there
ที่นี่	tîi-nîi	here
ที่ราบ	tîi-ráap	plain
ที่ล้างรถ	tîi láang rót	car wash
ที่อยู่	tîi yùu	address
ทุกๆ คน	túk túk kon	everyone
ทุกๆ ปี	túk túk bpii	every year
ทุกวัน	túk wan	every day
ที่เป่าผม	tîi bpào pǒm	hair dryer
ที่เปิดขวด	tîi bpùrd kùat	bottle-opener
ที่จอดรถ	tîi jòrd rót	car park
ที่บังแดด	tîi-bang-dàet	sunshade
ทีม	tiim	team (football, etc.)

Thai	Transliteration	English
หีบรับกระเป๋า	tîi ráb grà-bpǎo	baggage reclaim
เดินทาง	dum taang	
ทุกทุก วัน	túk túk wan	every day
โทรตางประ	too dtaang bpra	international
โทรศัพท์	tèet	call
โทรทัศน์	too-rá-tát	television
โทรศัพท์	too-rá-sàp	phone
โทรหา	too-hǎa	to call (on phone)
ทะเล	tà-lee	sea
ทะเลสาบ	tà-lee sàap	lake
ทัวร์	tuaa	tour
ทัวร์นำเที่ยว	tuaa nam tîao	guided tour
แท็กซี่	táek-sîi	taxi
มิเตอร์แท็กซี่	mi-dtur-táek-sîi	meter (taxi)
เทปเพลง	téep-pleeng	tape (cassette)
เที่ยงคืน	tîang kuun	midnight
เทียน	tian	candle
แท้	táe	genuine
โทร	too	to telephone
โทรศัพท์	too-rá-sàp	telephone

Thai – English

Thai – English

เท้า	táao	foot
ธ	tur	she
ธรรมดา	tam-mà-daa	simple
ธันวาคม	tan-waa-kom	December
เหล็ก	táat lèk	iron (mineral)
เตารีด	dtao-rîit	iron
น		
นมสด	nom sòt	fresh milk
นอน	nom	to sleep
นักหนังสือ	nák-nǎng-sǔu-	journalist
พิมพ์	pim	
นั้น	nán	that
น่าเกลียด	nâa-gìat	ugly
นาที	naa-tii	minute
นาน	naan	long
นามสกุล	naam-sà-gun	surname
นำ	nam	bring
น้ำ	náam	water
น้ำแกง	náam-gaeng	mineral water

น้ำแอปเปิล	náam apple	apple juice
น้ำกลั่น	náam glàn	distilled water
น้ำจิ้ม	náam jîm	sauce
น้ำดื่ม	náam dùum	drinking water
น้ำตก	náam dtòk	waterfall
น้ำตาล	náam dtaan	sugar
น้ำตาลเทียม	náam dtaan tiam	sweetener
น้ำผึ้ง	náam-pûng	honey
น้ำมะเขือเทศ	náam má-kǔa-têet	tomato juice
น้ำมัน	náam man	oil
น้ำมันรถ	náam man rót	petrol
น้ำสะอาด	náam sà-aat	fresh water
น้ำหนัก	náam nàk	weight
น้ำหนึ่งแก้ว	náam nùng gâew	a glass of water
น้ำหอม	náam hǒm	perfume
น้ำหนึ่งขวด	náam nùng kùat	a bottle of water
น้ำส้ม	náam sôm	orange juice
น้ำยาทาเล็บ	náam-yaa-taa-lép	nail polish

Thai		English
น้ำมันมะกอก	náam man mà-gò;k	olive oil
น้ำผลไม้	náam pôhn-la-máai	fruit juice
น้ำชา	náam-chaa	tea
น้ำแข็ง	náam kǎeng	ice
น้ำแข็งเปล่า	náam kǎeng bplàao	iced water
น้ำแร่	náam râe	mineral water
น้ำมะเขือเทศ	náam-má-kǔa-têet	tomato juice
น้ำมะนาว	náam ma-naow	lemonade
น้ำยาล้างเล็บ	náam-yaa-láang lép	nail polish remover
น้ำยาซักผ้า	náam yaa sák pâa	washing powder
นาฬิกา	naa-li-gaa	clock
นาฬิกาปลุก	naa-li-gaa-bplùk	alarm clock
น่ารัก	nâa-rák	lovely
นั่ง	nâng	sit
น้องสาว	nóng sǎao	younger sister
นก	nók	bird

Thai		English
นมผง	nom-pǒng	powdered milk
นักศิลปะ	nák sǐn-lá-bpà	artist
หนัง	nǎng	cinema
หนังสือ	nǎng-sǔu	book
หน้าร้อน	nâa rórn	summer
หนาว	nǎao	cold
หนึ่งโหล	nùng-lǒo	dozen
นิ่ง	nîng	still (still water)
นิดหน่อย	níd-nòi	a little
นิดหน่อย	níd-nòi a little	bit
นิ่ม	nîm	soft
นิวซีแลนด์	niu-sii-laen	New Zealand
นี่	nîi	this
นักท่องเที่ยว	nák tô;ng-tîao	tourist
นมพร่องมันเนย	nom pro;ng man neei	skimmed milk
นม	nom	milk
เนื้อวัว	núa-wua	beef
แนะนำ	nâe-nam	to recommend

Thai – English

Thai – English

นาฬิกาข้อมือ	naa-lí-gaa kôr muu	watch (wrist)
เนื้อลูกวัว	núa lôok wua	veal
หน้ารัก	nâa-rák	pretty
น้ำผลไม้สด	náam-pôhn-lá-mái	fruit juice
น้ำผึ้งพระ จันทร์	náam pûng prá-jan	honeymoon
นิทัศการ	ní-tát-sà-gaan	exhibition
บวม	buam	swollen (finger, ankle, etc.)
บริติช	bri-tish	British
บริการ	bo-rí-gaan	service
ใบเสร็จ	bai-sèt	receipt
โบสถ์	bòot	church
แบน	baen	flat
แบตเตอรี่รถ	bàet-dtur-rîi-rót	battery (for car)
ถ่านไฟฉาย	tàan-fai-châai	battery (for torch, camera)
ใบขับขี่	bai-kàp-kìi	driving licence

เบนซินไร้สาร ตะกั่ว	ben-sin rái sǎan dta-gùa	unleaded petrol
เบียร์	beer	beer
เบียร์หนึ่งขวด	beer nùng kùat	a bottle of beer
เบียร์อีกขวด	beer ìik kùat	another beer
บน	bon	on
บน/ด้านขวา	bon/dâan kwǎa	on/to the right
บรั่นดี	brandy	brandy
บริเวณกางเต็นท์	bo-rí-ween kâai	camp site
บริการซักรีด	bo-rí-gaan sák-rîit	laundry service
บริษัท	bo-rí-sàt	company (business)
บริษัทท่องเที่ยว	bo-rí-sàt tô-ng-tîao	travel agent
บ่อย	bòi	often
บัตรโทรศัพท์	bàt too-rá-sàp	phonecard
บัตรผ่านประตู	bàt pàan bpra-dtuu	boarding card
บันได	ban-dai	stairs

Thai – English

Thai		English
เป็นเวลา	baang wee-laa	sometimes
บางใหม่	bâang mái	any
บางคน	baang kon	someone
บางอย่าง	baang yàang	something
บาง	baang	some
บาดเจ็บ	bàat jèb	injured
บ้าน	bâan	home, house
บ้านเช่า	bâan châo	guest-house
บ่าย	bàai	afternoon
บุคคล	bùk-kon	person
บุหรี่	bù-rìi	cigarettes
บริเวณค่าย อยู่ไหน?	bo-ri-ween kâai yùu nǎi?	where is the camp site?
บัตรประจำตัว	bàt bpra-jam-dtua	identification card
บ่ายนี้	bàai níi	this afternoon
บ่ายพรุ่งนี้	bàai prûng níi	tomorrow afternoon
บาร์	bar	bar
บินตรง	bin dtrong	direct flight

Thai		English
บิสกิต	bìt-gìt	biscuit
บุหรี่หนึ่งซอง	bù-rìi nùng soːng	biscuits / a packet of cigarettes
ใบรับรอง	bai-ráp-rorng	certificate
ใบส่งของ	bai-sòng-kôːng	invoice
ใบเก็บเงิน	bai-gèb ngum	bill
ใบราคา	bai raa-kaa	price list
ใบสั่งยา	bai-sàng yaa	prescription
ใบสะระแหน่	bai-sa-rà-nàe	mints
ใบสำเนา	bai-sǎm-nao	photocopy
เป็นเงิน	bùrng ngurn	to cash
บือ	bùa	bored (to feel)
ปิกนิก	bpìc-nìc	picnic
ปาก	bpàak	mouth
ป่วย	bpùai	ill
ฉันป่วย	chan bpùai	I am ill
ปลาหมึกยักษ์	bplaa-mùk-yák	octopus
ปลาสด	bplaa-sòt	fresh fish
ปลอดภัย	bplòrt pai	safe

Thai – English

Thai		English
บนสถานีรถ...	bpai tîi sà-tǎa-nii	to the station
เป็นไปได้	bpen bpai dâai	possible
เป็นไปไม่ได้	bpen bpai mâi dâai	impossible
เปิด	bpùrd	to switch on
ประตู	bpra-dtuu	door
ปวด	bpùat	ache
ป่า	bpàa	forest
โปรดปราน	bpròot-bpraan	favourite
ปลั๊ก	bplák	plug (electric)
เป้	bpêe	backpack
เปิด	bpùrd	to open
เปิด	bpùrd	to turn on
ปฐมพยาบาล	bpà-tǒm-pa-yaa-baan	first aid
บกติ	bpòk-gà-dtì	usually
ประเทศไอร์แลนด์	bprà-têet-ai-laen	Ireland
ประเพณี	bprà-pee-nii	tradition
ประกัน	bprà-gan	insurance
งานประชุม	gaan bprà-chum	conference

Thai		English
ประมาณ	bprà-maan	about
ปรารถนา	bpràad-ta-nâa	to prefer
ปราศจาก	bpràat-sa-jàak	without
		see GRAMMAR
ปราสาท	bpra-sàat	castle
ปล้น	bplôn	burglary
ปลาซาร์ดีน	bplaa-saa-diin	sardines
ปลาทูน่า	bplaa-tuu-nâa	tuna
ปลาหมึกตัว	bplaa mùk dtua	squid
เล็ก	lék	
ปวดฟัน	bpùat-fan	toothache
ปวดหัว	bpùat hǔa	headache
ปั๊มน้ำมัน	bpám náam man	petrol station
ปากกา	bpàak-gaa	pen
ป้ายรถเมล์	bpâai rót-mee	bus stop
ปาร์ตี้	bpaa-dtîi	party (celebration)
ปิ้ง	bpîng	toast
ปิงปอง	bping-bpoong	table tennis
ปิด	bpìd	shut
ปิด	bpìd	to switch off

ปิด	bpìd	to turn off (radio, light)
ปิด	bpìd	to close
ปิด	bpìd	closed
ปี	bpii	year
ปีนี้	bpii níi	this year
ปีหน	bpii mài	New Year
ปีน	bpiin	climbing
ประเทศออส เตรเลีย	bprà-têet-òt-sa-dtree-lia	Australia
ประเทศอิตาลี	bprà-têet-ì-dtaa-lii	Italy
ประจำวัน	bpra jam wan	daily
ประจำสัปดาห์	bprajam sàp-daa	weekly
ปลา	bplaa	fish
ปวดหัว	bpùat hŭa	headache
ป่วย	bpùai	ill
ปู่	bpùu	grandfather (paternal)
เปล	bplee	cot

เปลี่ยน	bplìan	to change (money)
เปลือกหอย	bplùak-hŏi	shell
เปียก	bpìak	wet
แปล	bplae	to translate
แป้ง	bpâeng	flour
ไปรษณียบัตร	bprai-sa-nii-ya-bàt	postcard
ผู้สูงอายุ	pôo sŭung aa-yú	senior citizen
ผ้าเช็ดมือ	pâa chét muu	hand towel
ผลัก	plàk	to push
แผ่นไม้	pàen mái	wood (substance)
แผนที่	pàen-tîi	map
แผ่นดินไหว	pàen-din-wâi	earthquake
ผิวไหม้แดด	piu mâi dàet	sunburn
ผงซักฟอก	póng-sák-fó:k	detergent
ผลไม้	pŏnla-mái	fruit
ผลไม้สด	pŏnla-mái sòt	fresh fruit
ผอม	pŏrm	thin

Thai – English

Thai – English

Thai		English
ผักใบเขียว	pàk-bai-kǐao	green leaves (vegetable)
ผ้าเช็ดปาก	pâa chét bpàak	napkin
ผ่านไปแล้ว	pàan bpai láew	ago
ผ้าปูเตียง	pâa-bpuu-dtiang	sheet (for bed)
ผ้าปูที่นอน	pâa-bpuu-tîi-nom	bedclothes
ผ้าลินิน	pâa linin	linen
ผ้าห่ม	pâa-hòm	blanket
ผิด	pìd	wrong
ผิว	pǐu	skin
ผื่น	pùun	rash (skin)
ผู้โดยสาร	pûu duoy sǎan	passenger
ผู้ใหญ่	pûu yài	adult
ผู้ชาย	pûu chaai	man
ผู้มาเยี่ยม	pûu maa vîam	visitor
ผู้หญิง	pûu-yǐng	woman
เผ็ด	pèt	spicy
แผลพุพอง	plǎe pú-po:ng	blister
ผม	pǒm	hair
ผัก	pàk	vegetable
ผักสด	pàk sòt	fresh vegetables
ผ้าเช็ดตัว	pâa chét dtua	towel
ผ้าพันแผล	pâa-pan-plǎe	bandage
ผึ้ง	pûng	bee
ผู้จัดการ	pûu-jàt-gaan	manager
ผู้นำทาง	pûu nam tuaa	a guide
ผู้ปกครอง	pûu bpòk-krong	parents
ฝาก	fàak	deposit
ฝน	fǒn	rain
ฝักบัว	fàk bua	shower (bath)
ฝั่งทะเล	fàng-tà-lee	coast
พูด	pûud	to say
พุดดิ้ง	púd-dîng	pudding
พิเศษ	pí-sèet	special
พักผ่อน	pák pò:n	to rest
พ่อ	pôr	father
พวกเขา	pûag-kǎo	they
พลาสติก	pláas-tìk	plastic

Thai – English

Thai	Transliteration	English
พี่ชาย	pîi-chaai	brother
พูด	pûud	to speak
ฟองน้ำ	fo:ng náam	sponge (for cleaning)
ไฟลวกมือฉัน	fai-lûak-muu-chan	I've burned my hand
ไฟแช็ก	fai-sháek	lighter (cigarette)
แฟน	faen	boyfriend
แฟลต	flat	flat (apartment)
ฟิล์ม	film	film
ฟ้า	fáa	blue
ฟันปลอม	fan-bplorm	dentures
ฟัน	fan	teeth
เฟอร์นิเจอร์	fur-ni-jûr	furniture
การชำระภาษีเพิ่ม	paa-sǐi-muun-la-kâa-pûrm	VAT
ภาพวาด	pâap-wâad	painting (picture)
ภรรยา	panrayaa	wife

Thai	Transliteration	English
ภูมิแพ้	puum-páe	allergy
ภูเขา	puu-kǎo	mountain
ภาพ	pâap	picture (on wall)
มีประโยชน์	mii-bprà-yòot	useful
มีดโกน	mîit-goon	razor
มิถุนายน	mí-tù-naa-yon	June
มากไป	mâak bpai	too much
มาก	mâak	very
มันเสีย	man sǐa	this is off (milk, food)
ไม่มีอะไรๆ	mâi mii a-rai	nothing
ไม้ขีด	máai-kìit	matches (light)
ไม่	mâi	no
ไม่เคย	mâi keei	never
แม่	mâe	mother
แมลง	ma-laeng	insect
แมว	maew	cat
มาถึง	maa tǔng	to come (arrive)
มัน	man	greasy

Thai	Roman	English
มด	mót	ants
มหาวิทยาลัย	má-hǎa-wít-ta-yaa-lai	university
มองหา	morng-hǎa	to look for
มะเขือเทศ	má-kǔa-têet	tomato
มะกอก	má-gòk	olives
มะพร้าว	má-práao	coconut
มังสวิรัติ	mang-sà-wí-rát	vegetarian
มัน	man	it
มันดีมาก	man dii mâak	it's very nice
มันติด	man dtit	it's stuck
ติด	dtìt	stuck
มันฝรั่งทอด	man-fa-ràng-tôrt	fried potatoes
มันฝรั่งบด	man-fa-ràng-bòd	mashed potato
มันปิดรึเปล่า?	man bpìd rúu bplàao?	is it closed?
มันฝรั่ง	man-fa-ràng	potato
มันฝรั่งทอดกรอบ	maan fa-ràng tôrt	chips
มันอายุกี่ปี?	man a-yú gìi bpii?	how old is it? (building, etc.)

Thai	Roman	English
ม้า	máa	horse
มาก	mâak	a lot
มากมาก	mâak mâak	lot
มาก	mâak	more
มาถึง	maa tǔng	to arrive
มัสตาร์ด	mát-sà-tàad	mustard
มีโทรศัพท์	mii too-rá-sàp	telephone call
มา	maa	
มีด	míit	knife
มีนาคม	mii-naa-kom	March
มีสระน้ำไหม?	mii sà-náam mái?	Is there a pool?
มืด	mûud	dark
มือ	muu	hand
มุ้ง	múng	mosquito net
มูลค่า	muun-la-kâa	value
มีตำหนิ	mii dtam-ni	fault (defect)
แม่ยาย	mâe-yaai	mother-in-law
ไม่สะดวก	mâi-sà-dùak	inconvenient
มีชื่อเสียง	mii chûu-sǐang	famous
เมื่อคืน	mûa kuun	last night

Thai – English

Thai – English

Thai	Romanization	English
เมื่อย	mûai	tired, stiff
เมษายน	mee-sǎa-yon	April
ยุ่ง	yûng	busy
ยุโรป	yú-rôop	Europe
ยานอนหลับ	yaa-nom-làp	sleeping pill
ยาก	yâak	difficult
ยา	yaa	pill
เยี่ยม	yîam	to visit
ยกเลิก	yók-lôrk	cancel
ยา	yâa	grandmother (paternal)
ยาแก้ปวด	yaa-gâe-bpùat	painkiller
ยาก	yâak	hard (tough)
ยาคุมกำเนิด	yaa-kum-gam-nùrt	contraceptive pill
ยาฆ่าเชื้อโรค	yaa-kâa-chúa-rôok	disinfectant
ย่าง	yâang	grilled
ยาสีฟัน	yaa-sǐi-fan	toothpaste

Thai	Romanization	English
ยินดีต้อนรับ	yindii dtôːn ráb!	welcome!
ยิ้ม	yím	smile
ยุง	yung	mosquitoes
ยอดเยี่ยม	yôrt-yîam	excellent
ยางยืด	yaang-yûud	elastic band
แยกกัน ๆ	yâek gan	separately
รายการไวน์	raai-gaan wine	wine list
ร้านขายของฝาก	ráan kǎai kǒːng fàak	souvenir shop
ราชินี	raa-chi-nii	queen
ระเบียบข้อบังคับ	rá-bìap kôr bang-káp	regulations
รองเท้าแตะ	rorng-táao-dtàe	sandals
รองเท้า	rorng-táao	shoes
รถเข็น	rót-kěn	wheelchair
รถเข็น	rót-kěn	pushchair
โรงเรียน	roong-rian	school
เร็ว	reo	fast

Thai	Transliteration	English
เรา	rao	we
เรือ	ruua	ship
เรือเล็ก	ruua lék	dinghy
รถยนต์	rót	car
รถไฟ	rót-fai	train
รถไฟเที่ยวแรก	rót fai tîao râek	the first train
รถไฟใต้ดิน	rót fai dtâi din	underground (metro)
รถตู้	rót dtûu	van
รถบรรทุก	rót-ban-túk	truck
รถเมล์	rót-bus	bus
รถเมล์เที่ยวแรก	rót-bus tîao râek	the first bus
รวมทั้งหมด	ruam-táng-mót	total
รวย	ruai	rich (person)
รหัสไปรษณีย์	ra-hàt too-rá-sàp	dialling code
รหัสไปรษณีย์	ra-hàt prai-sa-nii	zip code
รอ	ror	to wait (for)
รองเท้าแตะ	ro:ng-táao dtàe	slippers
ร้องไห้	ró:ng-hâai	to cry (weep)
ระบบเตือนภัย	ra-bòb-dtuan-pai	alarm system

Thai	Transliteration	English
รัก	rák	to love
รับ	ráb	to accept
ราคา	raa-kaa	cost
ราคา	raa-kaa	price
ร้าน	ráan	shop
ร้านเค้ก	ráan-cake	cake shop
ร้านเพลง	ráan pleeng	music shop
ร้านขายของขวัญ	ráan kǎai kǒ:ng-kwǎn	gift shop
ร้านซักแห้ง	ráan sák hâeng	dry-cleaner's
ร้านสินค้า ปลอดภาษี	ráan sin-káa bplòrt paa-sǐi	duty-free shop
ร้านหนังสือ	ráan nǎng-sǔu	bookshop
รายการ	raai-gaan	menu
รู้	rúu	to know
ระเบียง	ra-biang	terrace
โรคกลัวน้ำ	rôok-glua-náam	rabies
รู้สึก	rúu-sùk	feel
ร่ม	rôm	umbrella
เรือข้ามฟาก	ruua-kâam-fâak	ferry

Thai – English

Thai – English

เรือยอชต์	ruua yót	yacht
ลูกชาย	lûuk-chaai	son
ล้อเล่น	lór-lên	joke, to tease
ลมแรง	lom raeng	windy
เล็ก	lék	little (small)
ลิ้นชัก	lín-chák	drawer
ลายเซ็น	laai-sen	signature
ล่ามโซ่	lâam-sŏo	to chain
ล่าม	lâam	interpreter
ล้าง	láang	to wash
ล็อกเกอร์	lock-gur	locker (for luggage)
ล็อก	lock	lock
ลงรถ	long rót	to get off (bus, etc.)
ลงจอด	longjòrt	landing
ลึก	lúk	deep
ล่าช้า	lâa-cháa	delay
ลิปสติก	lip-sa-dtick	lipstick

ลูกเกด	lûuk gèet	raisins
ลูกเทนนิส	lûuk ten-nís	tennis ball
ลูกบอล	lûuk-bo:n	ball
ลูกสาว	lûuk săao	daughter
เล็ก	lék	small
เล็กกว่า	lék gwàa	smaller
เล่น	lên	to play
เล่นสเก็ต	lên sà-gèt	to skate
เลือด	lûat	blood
เลือดกรุ๊ป	lûat-group	blood group
เลือดออก	lûat òrk	to bleed
ว		
วัน	wan	day
วันเกิด	wan gùrt	birthday
วันเกิด	wan gùrt	date of birth
วันที่	wan tîi	date (calendar)
วันนี้	wan níi	today
วันหยุด	wan yùd	holiday
วันหยุดทั่วไป	wan yùd tûa bpai	public holiday
วันหลัง	wan lăng	later

Thai – English

Thai		
วันจันทร์	wan-jan	Monday
วันเสาร์	wan-săo	Saturday
วันพุธ	wan-pút	Wednesday
วันศุกร์	wan-sùk	Friday
วันพฤหัสบดี	wan-pá-rú-hàt-sa-bo:-dii	Thursday
วันอาทิตย์	wan aa-tít	Sunday
วันอังคาร	wan ang-kaan	Tuesday
วัด	wát	measure
ไวน์แดง	wine-daeng	red wine
ไวน์	wine	wine
เวรโรมดึก	ween-rôrb-dùk	night duty
เภสัชกร	pee-sàt-cha-gorn	chemist
วงจร	wong-jom	a cycle
ว่าง	wâang	free (unoccupied)
ว่างเปล่า	wâang bplào	empty
ว่างงาน	wâang ngaan	unemployed
ว่ายน้ำ	wâai-náam	to swim
วิทยุ	wit-ta-yú	radio
วินาที	vi-naa-tii	second
วีซ่า	vii-sâa	visa
วิตามิน	vi-dtaa-min	vitamin pills
วอลเลย์บอล	vol-lêe-bo:n	volleyball
ศุลกากร	sŭn-la-gaa-gorn	customs
ศูนย์กลาง	sŭun-glaang	central
ศาลากลาง	săa-la-glaang	town hall
ศูนย์	sŭun	zero
ศูนย์กลางเมือง	sŭun glaang muang	city centre
ศูนย์กลางเมือง	sŭun glaang muang	town centre
ศูนย์บริการฝ่ายท่องเที่ยว	sŭun bo:-ri-gaan nák-tô:ng-tîao	tourist office
เศร้า	săo	sad
เศษสตางค์	sèet-sa-dtaang	change (loose coins)

Thai	Transliteration	English
ซู	súung	tall
สีส้ม	sǐi sôm	orange (colour)
สีแดง	sǐi daeng	red
สำหรับขาย	săm-ràp kǎai	for sale
สาย	sǎai	late
สามี	sǎa-mii	husband
สั้น	sân	short
สั่งอาหาร	sàng aa-hǎan	to order (food)
สะกด	sà-gòt	spell
สลัดมันฝรั่ง	sà-làd man-fa-ràng	potato salad
สลัด	sà-làd	salad
สถานีรถไฟ	sà-tǎa-nii rót fai	railway station
สถานีสุนทรกลาง	sa-tǎa-nii sǔun-glaang	central station
สถานกงสุล	sà-tǎan-gong-sǔn	consulate
โสด	sòod	single
เสื้อ	sûa	shirt
เสื้อกันฝน	sûa gan fǒn	raincoat

Thai	Transliteration	English
เสื้อแจ็กเก็ต	sûa jáek-gét	jacket
เสื้อกันหนาว	sûa-gan-nǎao	sweater
เสื้อหนัง	sûa năng	leather jacket
เสื้อชูชีพ	sûa-chuu-chíip	life jacket
เสื้อผ้า	sûa pâa	clothes
เสื้อยืด	sûa yûud	t-shirt
เสื้อคลุม	sûa klum	coat
สก็อตแลนด์	sà-gót-laen	Scotland
สกีน้ำ	sà-gii náam	water-skiing
ส่ง	sòng	to send
สงคราม	sŏng-kraam	war
ส่งต่อ	sòng dtòr	forward(s)
สด	sòt	fresh
สเก็ต	sà-gét	skates
สมุนไพร	sà-mǔn-prai	herbs
สลัดผลไม้	sà-làd pŏnla-máai	fruit salad
สวน	sǔan	park
สวย	sǔay	beautiful
สวัสดี	sà-wad-dii	good day
สวิตช์	sà-wit	switch

Thai	Transliteration	English
สมบูรณ์แบบ	sǒm-buun-bàep	perfect
สถานทูต	sa-tǎan tûut	embassy
สถานทูตอังกฤษ	sa-tǎantûut ang-grìt	British embassy
สถานกงสุลอังกฤษ	sà-tǎan-gong-sǔn sǔn ang-grìt	British consulate
สถานกงสุลอเมริกา	sà-tǎan-gong-sǔn a-mee-ri-gaa	American consulate
สถานทูตอเมริกา	sa-tǎan tûut a-mee-ri-gaa	American embassy
สถานีตำรวจ	sà-tǎa-nii dtam-rùat	police station
สถานี	sà-tǎa-nii	station
สถานีรถไฟอยู่ที่ไหน	sà-tǎa-nii kón sòng yùu tîi nǎi?	where is the bus station?
สถานีดับเพลิง	sà-tǎa-nii-dàp-plung	fire brigade
สถานีรถไฟ	sà-tǎa-nii kón sòng	bus station
สนใจ	sǒn-jai	to be interested in
สนามเทนนิส	sà-nǎam ten-nís	tennis court
สนามกีฬา	sà-nǎam gii-laa	stadium
สนามบิน	sà-nǎam-bin	airport
สบาย	sà baai	comfortable
สบู่	sà-bùu	soap
ส้ม	sôm	orange
สมุดเช็ค	sà-mùt chéck	cheque book
สระน้ำ	sà-nǎam	pool
สระว่ายน้ำ	sà-wǎai nǎam	swimming-pool
สลัดมะเขือเทศ	sà-làd má-kǔa-têet	tomato salad
สวน	sǔan	garden
สวนบุคคล	sǔan bùk-kon	private
สวนลด	sǔan lód	discount
สวนสัตว์	sǔan sàt	zoo
สวัสดี	sà-wàd-dii	hello
สัปดาห์ที่แล้ว	sàp-daa tîi láew	last week
สากล	sǎa-gon	international

Thai – English

Thai		English
สำคัญ	sǎm-kan	important
สำหรับ	sǎm-ràp	for
สัญชาติ	sǎn-châat	nationality
สัญญาณ	sǎn-yaan	sign (road, notice, etc.)
สัญญาณไฟ	sǎn-yaan dtuan fai	fire alarm
สับ	sàp	chop (meat)
สัปดาห์	sàp-daa	week
สัปดาห์หน้า	sàp-daa nâa	next week
สามีของฉัน	sǎa-mii kǒng chan	my husband
สามีภรรยา	sǎamii-panrayaa	couple (two people)
สำนักงาน	sǎm-nák-ngaan	office
สิงหาคม	sǐng-hǎa-kom	August
สี	sǐi	colour
สีน้ำตาล	sǐi-náam-dtaan	brown
สีม่วง	sǐi mûang	purple
สุเหร่า	sù-rào	mosque
สุกสุก	sùk sùk	well done (meat)

Thai		English
สุขสันต์วันเกิด	sùk-sǎn wan-gùrt	Happy Birthday!
สูง	sǔung	high
สูตรอาหาร	sùut aa-hǎan	recipe
สูท	sùut	suit (clothes)
สูบบุหรี่	sùub bu-rìi	to smoke
เสร็จ	sèt	finish
สูงชัน	sǔung-chan	steep
สกปรก	sòk-gà-bpròk	dirty
สมุดโทรศัพท์	sà-mùt too-rá-sàp	directory (telephone)
สำหรับฉัน	sǎm-ràp chan	for me
เสียหาย	sǐa hǎai	damage
แสดง	sà-daeng	show
แสตมป์	sà-dtaem	stamp
หิว (น้ำ)	hǐu (náam)	thirsty
หายใจ	hǎai-jai	to breathe
หัวใจ	hǔa-jai	heart
ห้องว่าง	hông wâang	vacancy (room)
ห้องครัว	hông krua	kitchen

Thai	Transliteration	English
ห้องขายตั๋ว	hôːng kǎi dtǔa	box office
ห้องเดี่ยว	hôːng dìao	single room
หวี	wǐi	comb
หวัด	wàt	cold
หลังคา	lǎng-kaa	roof
หลอดไฟ	lòrd-fai	light bulb
หรือ	rǔu	or
หยุด	yùd	stop!
หยุด	yùd	quit
หนู	nǔu	rat
หนึ่ง	nùng	one
หนัง	nǎng	leather
ให้	hâi	to let (allow)
หูหนวก	hǔu-nùaak	deaf
หูเจ็บ	hǔu jèb	ear ache
หุ้นส่วน	hûn-sùan	partner (business)
หาย	hǎai	missing (thing)
ห้ามสูบบุหรี่	hâam sùub-bu-rìi	non-smoking
ห้างสรรพสินค้า	hâang sàp-pa-sǐn-káa	department store

Thai	Transliteration	English
หัวหอมใหญ่	hǔa-hǒːm-yài	onion
หัวมุม	hǔa mum	corner
หอย	hǒi	shellfish
ห้องอาหาร	hôːng aa-hǎan	restaurant
ห้องน้ำสุภาพสตรี	hôːng náam sù-pâap-sà-dtrii	ladies' (toilet)
ห้องนั่งรอ	hôːng nâng ror	waiting room
ห้องทานอาหาร	hôːng taan aa-hǎan	dining room
ห้องคู่	hôːng kûu	double room
ห้องแสดงศิลปะ	hôːng sa-daeng sǐn-lá-bpà	gallery (art)
ห้องเปลี่ยนเสื้อผ้า	hôːng bplìan sûa pâa	changing-room
ห้อง	hôːng	room
ห่อ	hòr	wrap
หลานสาว	lǎan-sǎao	niece
หลานชาย	lǎan-chaai	nephew
หลังจาก	paai-lǎng	after
หลัง	lǎng	back (of body)

Thai – English

Thai – English

Thai		English
หมายถึง	măai tŭng	mean
หมายเลข	măai lêk tà-bian	number plate
หมายเลขโทรศัพท์	măai lêk too-rá-sàp	phone number
หมากฝรั่ง	màak-fà-ràng	chewing-gum
หมั้น	mân	engaged (to be married)
หม้อ	môr	pot (for cooking)
หมวก	mùak	hat
หนู	nŏu	mouse
หน้า	nâa	face
หนังสือพิมพ์	năng-sŭu-pim	newspaper
หนังสือแนะนำ	năng-sŭu nǽe-nam	guide/guidebook
หนังสือเดินทาง	năng-sŭu dum taang	passport
หนัก	nàk	heavy
หน่วยกู้ภัย	nûai gôu pai	lifeguard
หนวด	nùat	moustache

Thai		English
หนวกหู	nùak hŭu	noisy
เหมือน	mŭan	same
หมดอายุ	mòt aa-yú	to expire
ใหญ่	yài	big
หมอน	mŏm	pillow
หมอฟัน	mŏr-fan	dentist
หนังสือโทรศัพท์	năng-sŭu too-rá-sàp	telephone directory
ห้องนอนเดี่ยว	hông-norn diao	single bedroom
หลอดไฟ	lòrd-fai	bulb (light)
หิว	hĭu	hungry
ฉันหิวข้าว	chan hĭu kâao	I'm hungry
อา	aa	aunt (father's younger sister)/
น้า	náa	(mother's younger sister)/
ป้า	bpâa	(parents' older sister)
อาหาร	aa-hăan	food

Thai	Romanization	English
อาหารหลัก	aa-hǎan-làk	main course (of meal)
อาหารเช้า	aa-hǎan cháao	breakfast
อาหารเย็น	aa-hǎan yen	evening meal
อาหารค่ำ	aa-hǎan kâm	dinner (evening meal)
อาหารทารก	aa-hǎan taa-rók	baby food
อาหารสำเร็จรูป	aa-hǎan sǎm-rèt-rûub	delicatessen
อีกครั้ง	ìik kráng	again
อีสุกอีใส	i-sùk-i-sǎi	chickenpox
อื่น	ùun ùun	other
อิสลาม	it-sà-laam	Muslim
อ่างล้างหน้า	àang láang nâa	washbasin
อ่างล้างจาน	àang láang jaan	sink
อัตรา	àt-dtraa	rate
ออกค่าย	òrk-kâai	to camp
ออกเรือ	òrk ruua	sailing
ออก	òrk	out
อนุญาต	à-nú-yâat	permit

Thai	Romanization	English
ไอศกรีม	ai-sa-kriim	ice cream
อก	òk	chest (of body)
อธิบาย	à-tí-baai	to explain
อพาร์ตเมนท์	a-páat-mén	apartment
อย่างเร็ว	yàang reo	quickly
อร่อย	aròy	tasty
อร่อย	aròy	delicious
อ้วน	ûan	fat (person)
ไขมัน	kài-man	fat (food)
ออก	òrk	out
ออกไป	òrk bpai	to go out
อักเสบ	àk-sèep	infection, to become inflamed
อังกฤษ	ang-grìt	England
อันไหน	an nǎi?	which one?
อันไหน	an nǎi?	which?
อากาศดี	aa-gàat dii	fine (weather)
อาบแดด	àap dàet	sunbathe
อายุ	aa-yú	age

Thai – English

Thai - English

Thai	Phonetic	English
อาศัย	aa-sǎi	to live
อาหาร	aa-hǎan	meal
อาหารกลางวัน	aa-hǎan glaang wan	lunch
อาหารทะเล	aa-hǎan tá-lee	seafood
อีเมล	e-mail	e-mail
อุโมงค์	ù-moong	tunnel
อุ่น	ùn	warm
อ่าน	àan	to read
เอ็กซเรย์	ék-sà-ree	x-ray
คนไอริช	kon-ai-rish	Irish
อันตราย	an-dta-raai	dangerous
อุบัติเหตุ	ù-bàt-dti-hèet	accident
อุณหภูมิ	un-hà-puum	temperature
อเมริกา	a-mee-ri-gaa	America
องุ่น	a-ngùn	grapes
อย่างไร?	yàang-rai?	how?
อย่างอื่น	yàang ùun	another
อยู่คนเดียว	yùu kon diao	alone
อะไร?	a-rai?	what
อัตราแลกเปลี่ยน	àt-dtraa lâek bplìan	exchange rate
แฮม	haem	ham

Further titles in Collins' phrasebook range
Collins Gem Phrasebook

Also available as **Phrasebook CD Pack**
Other titles in the series

Arabic	Greek	Polish
Cantonese	Italian	Portuguese
Croatian	Japanese	Russian
Czech	Korean	Spanish
Dutch	Latin American	Thai
French	Spanish	Turkish
German	Mandarin	Vietnamese